I0617428

A World Before Genesis: Ta-Seti, Kemet and The Nile Valley Kingdom: Volume 1

Published by Daniel Laroche MD

49 West 127th Street

New York, NY, 10027

Email: dlarochemd@gmail.com

Library of Congress Control Number: 2023915961

ISBN# 979-8-9851110-5-7

Published in the United States

Why this book?

Thank you for your support and your purchase of this book. I would like to share with you why I wrote it. This is not a book I could have written many years ago. Having years of life experiences, travels to continents and museums across the globe, and reading many books, I have learned a great deal of information and acquired knowledge. I have been very fortunate to read many books and visit several museums such as the Metropolitan Museum in NY, Brooklyn Museum in NY, Oriental Museum in Chicago, Louvre Museum in France, British Museum in England, Heritage Museum in Russia (St. Petersburgh), and the National Museum in Ethiopia. I have also traveled to Egypt (Kemet), Ethiopia, Rwanda, Kenya, Nigeria, South Africa, Haiti, Ghana and Jamaica. Throughout these learning experiences, I learned of the great origin of civilization from Africa, which I was never taught in school, growing up in New York in the United States.

The history of this book starts from over 7 million years ago with Tournai as the first woman from Chad. We all descend from the womb of an African woman. It is important for the world to know this history. The book will stop at 700 BCE, which is when the Europeans, Persians and Arabs unfortunately invaded Kemet, and this civilization became manipulated and whitewashed with Europeans and Arabs inserting themselves in African history and traditions.

In this book, I am sharing highlights of my travel, readings, teachings, and wisdom of our ancestors and my mentors. I'm making this information available to an audience who may not travel or have access to the many books I have read to compile this text. Many people may not have the opportunity to see these places and experience first-hand of the great African Kushite-Kemetic (ancient Egypt) origin and its contributions to civilization. This is very important information for everyone to know.

The content of this book is critical and essential for all developing minds. It is knowledge of the true history of civilization. It will give a much greater respect for the contributions to civilization of persons from African descent and how we all share the same goals of peace, harmony, truth, balance, order, reciprocity and propriety for success. Learning the history and teachings of our ancestors will lead to greater peace, success and understanding for all. I hope you enjoy this book. I hope it inspires, motivates and teaches you to pursue your passion with excellence, consistency, and persistency. It is my hope you will also share this beautiful history and legacy with others.

Sincerely,
Daniel Laroche, MD
Iry Imhotep Djehuty Anm-Ra

In the words of Dr. Ivan Van Sertima, it's best stated,

"We were trained to despise ourselves and all of Africa. We felt that Africans were either primitive or semi-primitive, that they had no science and made no significant contribution to civilization. We did not realize that we're looking at a looted Africa, a shattered Africa. We did not realize that there were two Africa's, Africa before and after the holocaust".

Quoted from the Ancestor Asa Hilliard

As a global scholar on African history, Asa Hilliard lectured all over the world. His research not only in his discourses but also in his books is synonymous with Ancient Kemet (Egypt). His findings set the tone for Volume I. During a television interview with Lestervelt Middleton, Asa Hilliard elaborates on Ancient Kemet, explaining:

We use the term Kemet instead of Egypt because that is the name the Kemetic people used to refer to themselves. The name Egypt was used by the Greeks and is a foreign name, not an African name.

Why is the study of ancient Kemet so important to the world and Black people in particular?

Kemet is important because it is humankinds' oldest civilization. This was developed by Africans. It is as important to Africans as Greece is important to Europeans. Kemet was a high technical civilization with many advances in sciences, writing, astronomy, music and many academic areas.

Who am I?

Where in the world am I?

How did I get here?

These are important questions for all Black youth to know the answers to, since they have not been properly taught in the European education system. Most well-developed nations spend billions of dollars answering these questions. This is invested in the form of libraries, universities, museums, and so forth. Without proper resources, African people are unable to preserve their rich history. It is essential to have the knowledge of one's history to obtain a strong sense of belonging. One's identity provides the basis for group unity which in return provides the basis for economic and political power.

The pattern of movement of people on the African continent starts from the White and Blue Nile north into Kemet. Then migration continues from Kemet to West Africa. The Dogan people in Mali have the same cultural and genetic connection from the Nile Valley.

If a group of people have no sense of being a part of the historical world, this has a negative effect on how they live their lives. When children learn the history about African people, they have an improvement in self-esteem and self-concept; improved attitudes occur nearly immediately. They will often develop a new mission and new purpose. This will often lead to a transformational experience in the child or adult.

Asa Hilliard Master keys on the interpretation of information from Kemet

Kemetic culture was predynastic. It remained the same for over 3000 years. This period may have been 5 – 20,000 years before the first dynastic period in 3000 BC. At 4246 BC, the calendar that we use now was already in place. The technology and mathematics back then were tremendous, and the culture was older than the politically formed society in Dynasty 1 [The time period of the first series of Nile Valley Kings to rule over a unified Egypt (Kemet). It immediately follows the unification by the first King Narmer]. The origins of the culture were in Central Africa known as Ta Seti [Upper and Lower Egypt by the first King Narmer].

Ta Seti, 3500 BC in Nubia, is another old civilization prior to Kemet and was led by Africans. Spirituality is already recorded by this time with astronomy, writing, Medu Netr, (hieroglyphic writing), and the God Heru is in place. Ausar is also in place as a God before organized political systems in Kemet. Ausar has the shepherd's crook and the flail.

The heka and nekhakha are the symbols of the crook and flail, which were very prevalent in ancient Kemetic (Egyptian) society. The crook represented kingship while the flail was for fertile earth. Initially, these symbols were associated with the qualities of Deity Ausar and later becoming an insignia of the pharaoh's authority.

He was the supreme God married to the virgin Auset. This was the first holy family that existed 3,000 years before the Christian story. Ausar was sacrificed by his brother Set and cut up in 14 to 28 pieces. He was remembered from the dead to rule over the deceased. The story of resurrection occurred 3,000 years before Christianity's Jesus Christ.

Kemetic culture remained intact through 700 century AD. At that time, the Africans were forcibly converted to Islam, and large numbers of

Arabic speaking people came in. This is what we see today.

The older things are the better– they are, and the oldest cultures were the better cultures. The older pyramids are better than the newer pyramids. The Giza pyramids from 2500 BC were the best, and the subsequent ones were less. The great pyramid is about 45 stories tall. The pyramid text on the tomb of Unas is the oldest spiritual document in the world. The book text is the Pert em Heru or The Book of Coming Forth by Day from Darkness of Night. The text was pure in written and symbolic form. The ideas were less contaminated with superstition. The Temple at Sakkara from 2700 BC by King Djoser has large round columns that were subsequently replicated at the Parthenon in Acropolis, Greece.

Although the Nile's outflux is downward from south to north, its directional orientation was up south. For the people of Kemet, the words left and east were the same while the words right and west were the same. Their general orientation was to the south with their backs to the north pole. Thus, the origin of the people and the culture is up south. There is a close connection between the Kemetic people and the Sudanese people. The cultural unity was between Kemet and the Africans. Significant leaders such as King Narmer were from up south near Luxor or Aswan.

The Dynasties of the four golden ages (Old Kingdom, Middle Kingdom, New Kingdom, and Late Kingdom) were from the south. The Imperial Age was centered at Waset, now known as Luxor. The Restoration Age was centered at Waset which the Greeks called Thebes. The Literary Age started at Waset and was the seat of Power. Waset, meaning the scepter, was the symbol of authority and power. The Literary Age started in Waset and was the home base of the preachers. The priests were the ones that disciplined royalty. The pharaoh did not have a free reign and had to gain approval from the priest; kings (pharaohs) could not rule alone.

Pharoah Djoser built the step pyramid, and the African ruler Mentuhotep reigned from Waset. Ahmenomet III fought in the Greek trojan war. Neferatari, Queen Mother Ahmose Nefertari, was part of Waset's leadership in the 18th Dynasty during the Age of architectural and imperial expansion. Ahmenohteop III and Queen Tiye with her husband ruled Kemet as a co-regent. She had many letters from foreign dignitaries and was the mother of Akhenaten, and possibly King Tut. The books that show pictures of white Egyptians are from the Greek and Roman time and thereafter.

All creativity is indigenous, and all of the invasions were destructive. The Persians in 525 BC and the Greco-Romans in 332 BC arrived to Kemet. The Romans that came in 30 BC destroyed the spiritual and educational institutions. Before they destroyed, they amassed all the great teachings of ancient Kemet (Egypt) and imitated.

The culture of ancient Kemet (area known as Egypt) from the Predynastic period (5500 BCE) to the Islamic conquest in 642 AD lasted more than 6,000 years. Egyptologists divided this 6,000-year period into 31 dynasties, grouped into Old, Middle and New Kingdoms. They also separated them by Intermediate Periods (First, Second and Third), which was followed by a Late Period (Samuel & Domain).

Table of Contents

Africa and the Nile Valley Landscape

Facts: Here is a map of Africa, the birthplace of civilization. These are the names of the territories before colonization *(the action or process of settling among and establishing control over the indigenous people of an area).* Civilization came to a zenith in Kemet and Kush. This area is today's Ethiopia, Sudan and Egypt.

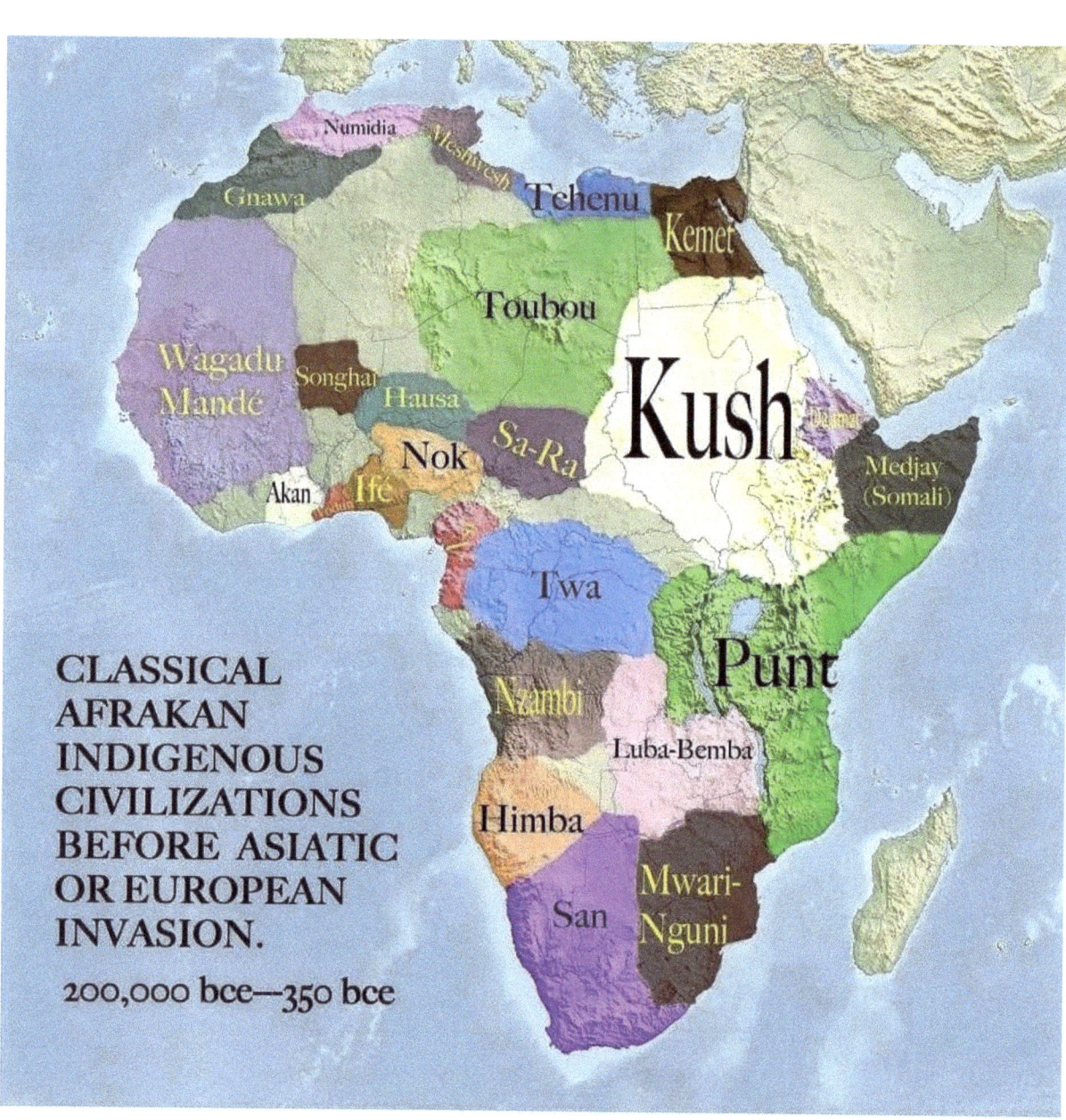

CLASSICAL AFRAKAN INDIGENOUS CIVILIZATIONS BEFORE ASIATIC OR EUROPEAN INVASION.

200,000 bce—350 bce

(Credit: Courtesy of Photographer Khonsu Nok)

Myth: Africa had no civilization.

Enlightenment: Africa is the origin of civilization, and the truth must be taught.

Facts: The below map zooms into the modern-day names of Kemet, now called Egypt with the cities and location. From Abu Simbel to Cairo, you will see the Nile River which is over 4,000 miles long and flows from south to north. The people referred to Upper Kemet, which is south where the Nile River originated (Leprohon).

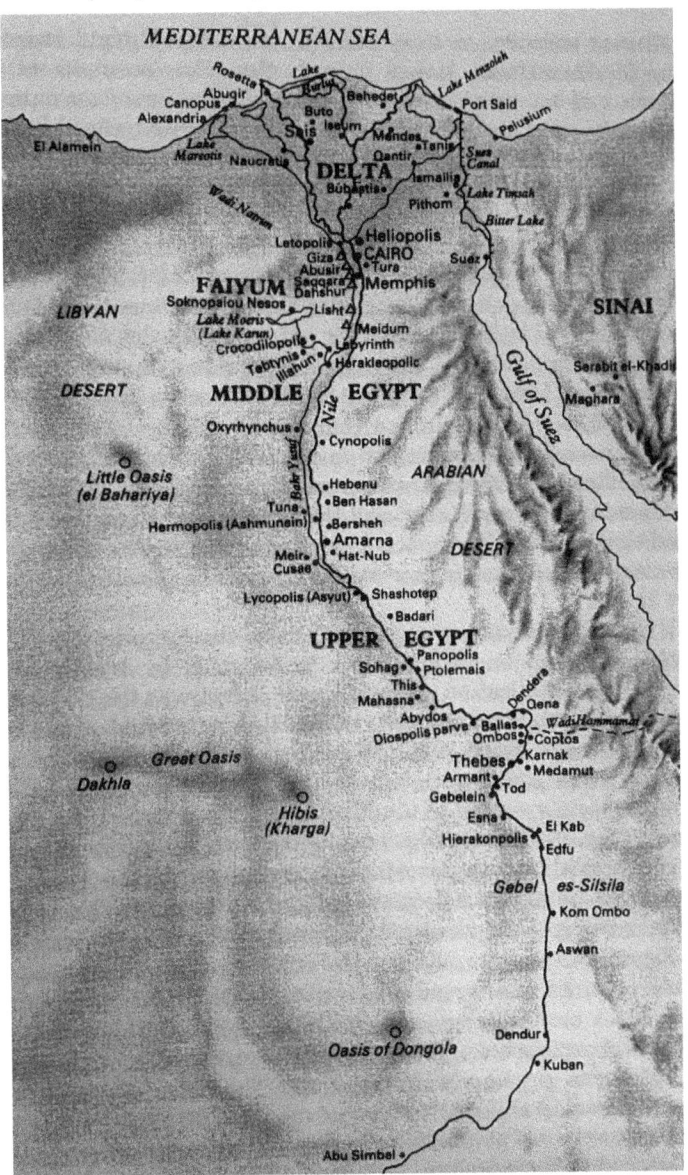

(Credit: Courtesy of Photographer Iwona Kozieradzka-Ogunmakin)

3

Myth: Egypt was the original name of this land.

Enlightenment: Kemet was the original name of this land prior to Greek and Arab invasions.

Facts: Nile River

The Nile is the Great River that has been providing life to this area. The Nile Valley has been carved by the passage of the river, driving northward from Central Africa and Ethiopia over many thousands of years and formed by a series of drainage systems that have found their ways to the sea.

The Nile River is fed by three main tributaries: the parent stream, the White Nile, rising in Lake Victoria; the smallest stream, the Atbara, joining the river above the Fifth Cataract near Berber; and the Blue Nile, joining Khartoum in Sudan that gives the river its character.

The Blue Nile rises in Lake Tana in Ethiopia. As it sweeps northwards, it carries alluvial silt with it. Once passes the six cataracts, it flows into the plain of Egypt, flooding the riverbanks. As it recedes, it leaves behind a rich belt of fertile silt which the ancient Egyptians called Kemet (the black land). As it continues northward, the torrent of the river slows and fans out to form the Delta. From Aswan, the Nile flows between cliffs, forming the boundaries of the valley. When it reaches Cairo, it divides north-east to Damietta and the sea, and northwest to Rosetta.

Within this bounteous patch, the twin rivers create four large sheets of water: Lakes Burollos, Idku, Mariout and Manzala. Only in 1971 was the water of the Nile partially tamed. The building of the High Dam in Aswan completely controls the river as it holds back the annual flood water. Consequently, it has helped to create the largest man-made lake in the world. Unfortunately, this decision by modern-day leaders of Egypt flooded and destroyed large areas of Nubia, including rich areas of artifacts that contributed to civilization (Ahmed).

(Photo credit: Public domain Wikipedia commons, Satellite image of Kemet)

Prehistoric Era

Facts: The oldest human bones are of "Lucy" who is from Kush which is now known as Ethiopia. With a hundred pieces of fossilized bones, 40% of the assembled skeleton is also known as Dinkinesh, meaning "you are marvelous" in the Ethiopian, Amharic language. The bones date to about 3.2 million years ago. The skeleton presents a small skull and evidence of an upright walking-gait (Dr. Y). This can be seen in the National Museum of Ethiopia.

(Photo credit: Daniel Laroche, National Museum Ethiopia, Ethiopia, Africa)

Myth: Adam and Eve were the first people on earth.

Enlightenment: This hard evidence demonstrates that Lucy is the ancestor of the entire human species. *Facts:* The first recorded civilization started in Africa in the Nile Valley about 200,000 years ago. The earliest drawings were on stones of animals from Africans, 25,000 – 36,000 years ago. At the Museum of Namibia, Nubian impressions depict a bow above a rectangle, probably the earliest writing to Ta-Seti.

Early Cave Drawings

(Image courtesy of State Museum of Namibia, Namibia, Africa)

Facts: The Lebombo bone was constructed from the fibula bone of a baboon's leg to make tools. The incised markings were detected in the Lebombo Mountains, located between South Africa and Eswatini. Based on 24-radiocarbon dating, they are approximately 44,200 to 43,000 years old and far older than the Ishango bone, which sometimes mistakenly is considered older than the Lebombo bone (Beaumont, 69: 41–46). According to The Universal Book of Mathematics, the Lebombo bone's 29 notches suggest "it may have been used as a lunar phase counter, in which case

African women may have been the first mathematicians, because keeping track of menstrual cycles requires a lunar calendar" (Darling).

Lebombo bone
(35,000 - 30,000 BC)

Ishango bone
(~22,000 BC)

(Photo credit: J.D. Loreto and D.H. Hurlbert, Smithsonian)

Myth: Africans did not contribute to mathematics.

Enlightenment: Africa is where mathematics began.

Facts: In the Democratic Republic of Congo, the Ishango bone was unearthed in the fisherman township of Ishango. The Ishango bone is curved, dark-brown colored and approximately 10 centimeters in length. It probably was used as a mathematical instrument that dates to the Upper Paleolithic. Scientists are unable to ascertain the animal the bone was extracted from because it had been scraped, narrowed, engraved, and polished, creating distortion.

The engraving marks are filled with important significance that includes astrological and mathematical interpretations. In a series of three columns, the markings extend the length of the bone and are viewed as a tally stick. They seem deliberate for counting and calculating basic mathematics. Dating as far back as 20,000 years ago, the Ishango bone is considered the oldest mathematical device in human history, with the exception of the Southern African Lebombo bone that is approximately 40,000 years old. Courtesy of Professor de Heinzelin, the Ishango bone currently is preserved at the Royal Belgian Institute of Natural Sciences. No longer on display for public viewing, interested parties must request in writing for face-to-face contact. The artifact is vulnerable and fragile, so mold copies were formed from petrified bone to transport to Brussels, Belgium at the

Royal Belgian Institute of Natural Sciences.

Interpretations

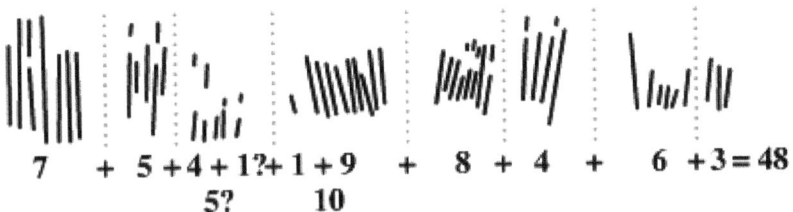

$$7 + 5 + 4 + 1? + 1 + 9 + 8 + 4 + 6 + 3 = 48$$
$$5? \quad 10$$

First (sometimes called "center") column (invisible in picture), from bottom to top

$$9 + 19 + 21 + 11 = 60$$

Second (or "right") column (to the left in picture), from bottom to top

$$19 + 17 + 13 + 11 = 60$$

Third (or "left") column (to the right in picture), from bottom to top

(Photo Credit: Wikipedia Commons, IshangoColumnA.png)

The bone comprises of 168 etch markings in three separately aligned columns with each etching, varied in length orientation Professor de Heinzelin believes the markings on the Ishango bone were deliberate and evidence of arithmetic. Based on archaeological findings, Professor de Heinzelin compared the Ishango "harpoon heads" to the bones excavated in northern Sudan and ancient Kemet (Egypt), which exposed the possible correlation between arithmetic functions with the Ishango bone and mathematics. (Royal Belgian Institute of Natural Sciences).

Drawing of the People, Animals, and Agriculture

PHOTO CREDIT: REUTERS, COURTESY OF PHOTOGRAPHER MOHAMED ABD EL GHANY

Facts: Over time, rock art became more elaborate and evolved. One of the earliest pottery artifacts is the incense burner of Qustul from Nubia in Africa on exhibit at the Oriental Museum, located in Chicago, Illinois. Crafted in Nubian rock art, the incense burner includes art designs on the rim, attributed to distinct Nubian style. The burner was discovered in the tomb of a Nubian leader at Qustul. With images aligned with Kemetic kings such as sacred boats, serekh palace façade, falcon deity, and White Crown of Upper Egypt, they symbolize the royal procession ritual by boat to the fortress.

(Photo credit: Daniel Laroche, Oriental Museum, Chicago, Illinois)

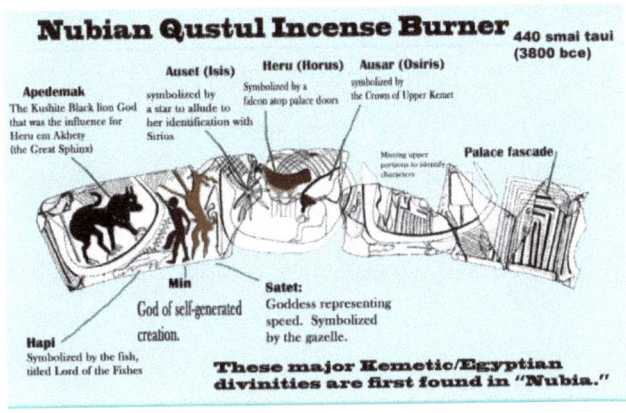

(Photo credit: Courtesy of Photographer Khonsu Nok)

Myth: Jesus, Mary and the Father were the first trilogy.

Enlightenment: The Ausar, Auset and Heru spiritual trilogy predates Jesus by thousands of years.

(Photo credit: Cush https://en.wikipedia.org/wiki/File:NC_Punt.jpg)

Facts: In ancient Kemetic (Egyptian) writings, Punt was abundant in resources and characterized as "the land of the Gods". In these inscriptions, evidence points to Puntland region of modern-day Somalia. The Puntland is famously known for the exploration of Queen Hatshepsut in 1493 BCE during the 18th Dynasty of Egypt. Kemet and Punt collaborated to import live trees to Kemet, which was acclaimed as the first successful endeavor at transplanting foreign fauna. Although this exchange is the most recognizable according to historical research, trade between the two dates as far back to the Fourth Dynasty (c. 2613 – 2498 BCE), and possibly earlier, which was during the leadership of pharaoh Khufu.

As Kemet expanded in trade, particularly with Punt and Nubia, they grew as a nation during the latter of the Predynastic Period (6000 – 3150 BCE). Punt was not only an important partner in trade with Kemet but also a source of religious and cultural impact. Kemetians viewed Punt as a land blessed by the Gods. The culture of modern-day Puntland, State of Somalia, has several similarities to ancient Kemet, including arts, language as well as ceremonial dress (Mark, "Punt").

Bes Twa

Twa the first people deified as Gods. Here is an image of Bes who was considered a deity.

(Photo credit: Daniel Laroche, Metropolitan Museum)

(Photo credit: Daniel Laroche, Nile Delta, Kemet)

(Photo credit: Courtesy of Photographer Juergen Ritterbach)

Myth: Pygmies contributed nothing to civilization.

Enlightenment: African Batwa Pygmies were the first people that helped to develop civilization.

14

Archaic Period Dynasty 1

Naqada Period Pottery 3600 BCE

Facts: Pots are like data; they provide insight into the cultural interchanges of African societies: the life they led, the paths they trod, the needs they had, and the skills they possessed. What do you learn from these pots? What do you see?

(Photo credit: Daniel Laroche, Metropolitan Museum)

(Photo credit: Daniel Laroche, Metropolitan Museum, Kemet)

(Photo credit: Daniel Laroche, Metropolitan Museum, Kemet)

18

(Photo credit: Daniel Laroche, Metropolitan Museum, Kemet)

(Photo credit: Daniel Laroche Metropolitan Museum, Kemet)

Myth: Africans contributed nothing to the Arts.

Enlightenment: Africans invented the Arts.

Facts: Currently on display at the Ashmolean Museum in Oxford, the Scorpion Macehead is another vital artifact. Made from limestone, it carries the appellation of a king Scorpion. It was found in pieces during the archaeological excavation of Hierakonpolis (originally Nekhen) and dates to the early Dynastic Period. The macehead was restored to its full size, approximately 25 centimeters high. Both weight and size suggest that its purpose was ceremonial in nature rather than daily use. The detailed-carved decoration of the macehead has fueled the controversy surrounding the alleged unification of Upper and Lower Kemet (Kinnaer, "Ancient Egypt").

(Photo credit: Baines-Malek, Atlas van het Oude Egypte, p. 79.)

21

Detailed Close up of the Macehead of King Scorpion Holding a Hoe
(Photo: Ashmolean Museum, Oxford, Wikipedia Commons)

The central figure displayed on the Macehead showcases King Scorpion. It is believed to be King Scorpion because of the floral design in front of him. Crowned in the white head dress, typically affiliated with Upper-Kemet, an animal's tail protrudes from the back of his tunic. Holding a hoe in his hands, King Scorpion is ready to open the earth. A man stands before him, releasing sand.

This representation portrays the pharaoh preparing the earth for a structure. An isle of liquid suggests King Scorpion probably was breaking ground for a dike or dam foundation. This is uncertain because there is no information of that timeframe that would reveal the actual location of such dike or dam. This traditional description is recognized throughout the history of the pharaohs. Scorpion Macehead

In the drawing, two of the king's subjects are fanning the king to keep him cool; they are surrounded by plants in a marsh. Two of the men are in front of him, symbolizing territorial borders of the king's monarchy. The level immediately above the king signifies a person seated while the lower level incorporates women dancing and patting their hands together. At the very top of the drawing are standards with birds hanging by the neck from each standard, representing the word people. Perhaps, it reflects the king's conquered territories and human subjects. King Scorpion was viewed as a warrior-king (Wikipedia, "Scorpion II").

Reconstructed Drawing of the Scorpion Macehead

(Photo **Source:** Adams-Cialowicz, *Protodynastic Egypt*, p. 8.)

Myth: Africans did not have organized governments or heads of state such as Kings and Queens. Enlightenment: The concept of Kings and Monarchs started in Africa.

Facts: In Kemet, we also find the world's first historical document which is the Palette of Narmer. This was written in stone on both sides. Narmer is said to be the son of Scorpion (Kinnaer, "The Narmer Palette").

24

The Narmer Palette

(Photo credit: Daniel Laroche, Egyptian Museum, Cairo, Kemet)

Dating back approximately to 3100 BCE, the Narmer Palette holds several of the earliest medu neter (hieroglyphic) writings to be found. It illustrates archetypal customs of Ancient Kemetic art which suggests art probably already was established prior to the creation of the Narmer Palette.

One of the most significant inclusions in the Narmer Palette describes Lower and Upper Kemet (Egypt) coming together under the ruler of King Narmer. He was one of the earliest Kemetic (Egyptian) kings represented in hieroglyphic inscriptions. On one side of the inscription, the king is adorned with a White Crown, representing southern Egypt (Upper), and the other side, he wears a Red Crown, representing northern, Lower Egypt (Kinnaer, "The Narmer Palette").

Palette of Narmer

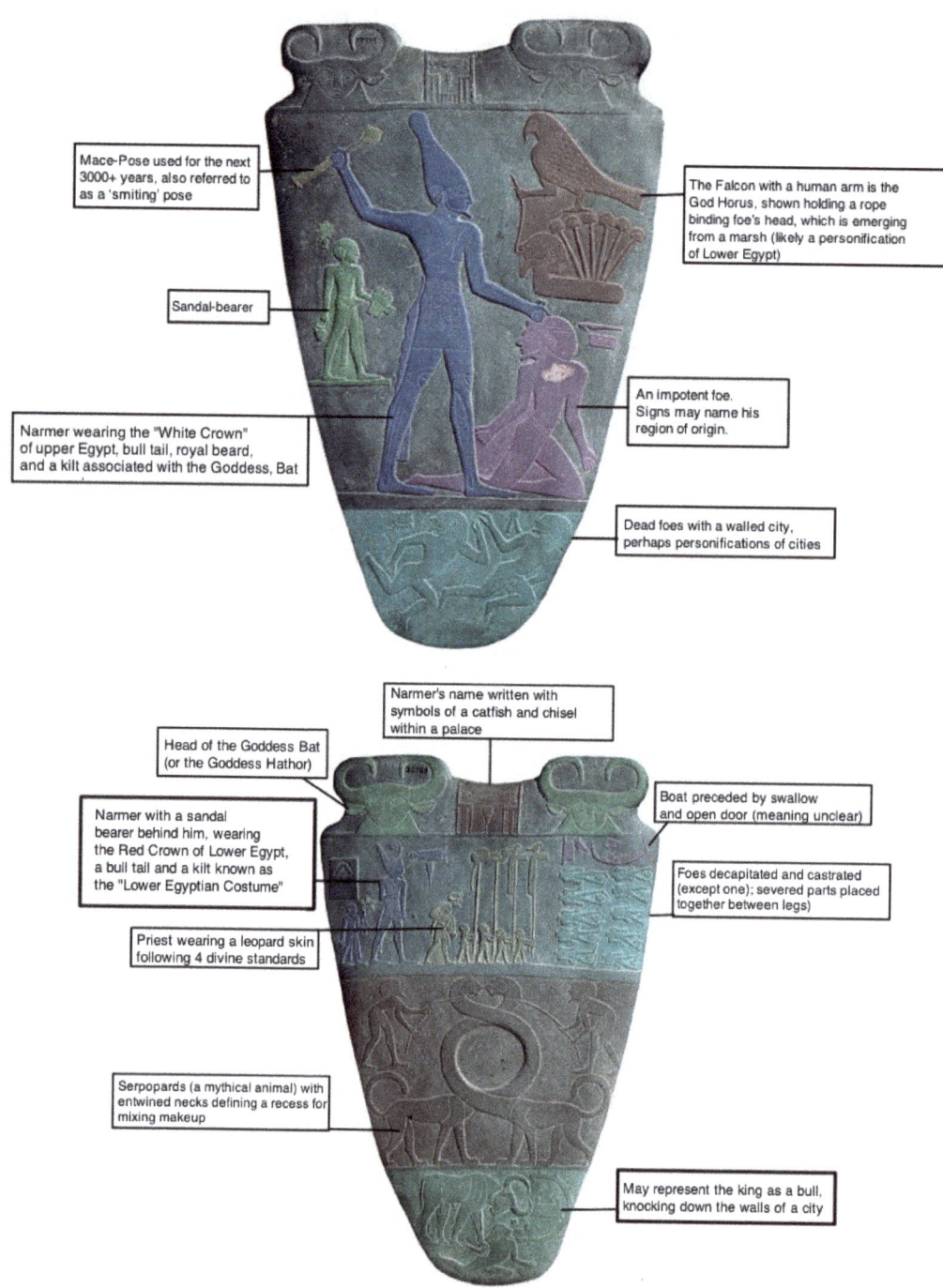

Mace-Pose used for the next 3000+ years, also referred to as a 'smiting' pose

The Falcon with a human arm is the God Horus, shown holding a rope binding foe's head, which is emerging from a marsh (likely a personification of Lower Egypt)

Sandal-bearer

Narmer wearing the "White Crown" of upper Egypt, bull tail, royal beard, and a kilt associated with the Goddess, Bat

An impotent foe. Signs may name his region of origin.

Dead foes with a walled city, perhaps personifications of cities

Narmer's name written with symbols of a catfish and chisel within a palace

Head of the Goddess Bat (or the Goddess Hathor)

Boat preceded by swallow and open door (meaning unclear)

Narmer with a sandal bearer behind him, wearing the Red Crown of Lower Egypt, a bull tail and a kilt known as the "Lower Egyptian Costume"

Foes decapitated and castrated (except one); severed parts placed together between legs)

Priest wearing a leopard skin following 4 divine standards

Serpopards (a mythical animal) with entwined necks defining a recess for mixing makeup

May represent the king as a bull, knocking down the walls of a city

(Photo credit: Egyptian Museum, Cairo, Kemet)

Myth: Africans did not excel in scholarship, culture, or the arts.

Enlightenment: Africans were the authors of the world's, first historical document.

26

Facts: King Narmer, also known as Menes by the Greeks, is viewed as the pharaoh (king) who built one of the greatest civilizations known to exist (Hayes, vol. I, pt. I, p. 24, Ch. VI). Petrie Museum of Egyptian Archaeology in London, England houses the below limestone of King Narmer.

(Photo credit: Courtesy of Photographer Osama Shukir Muhammed Amin, FRCP)

OLD KINGDOM

Spirituality of MA'AT

Facts: From the Nubian Museum are images below of women with a feather in their head, representing MAAT.

(Photo credit: Daniel Laroche, Nubian Museum, Public Domain)

(Photo credit: Daniel Laroche, Nile River Valley, Kemet)

Spelled either Ma'at or Maat, the teachings of Maat were seen in the earliest surviving pyramid texts in Africa, dating back to the Old Kingdom, 2375 BCE to 2345 BCE. They are on the sarcophagi (tombs) as well as the pyramid walls at Saqqara, dating back to the 5th and 6th Dynasties of the Old Kingdom (2613 BCE to 2181 BCE).

This Ancient Kemetic word Maat incorporates seven concepts of high value: "truth, balance, order, harmony, law, morality, and justice". Maat is esteemed to the embodiment of all seven principles. Pharaohs (nst bity/ kings) sometime were adorned with the insignias of Maat, stressing the importance of righteousness and laws. During the early reign of kings, they ruled through the authority of Maat and were the "Lord of Maat", decreeing from their mouth and heart the conception of Maat. From the Eighteenth Dynasty (1550 BCE – 1295 BCE), Maat was viewed as Ra's daughter (Strudwick, pp. 106 – 107).

Traditionally represented as a woman with a feather in her hair, Maat is considered the Neter (divine concepts and principles) who created order out of disorder as opposed to her arch opposite Isfet, the god of evil, chaos, injustice and violence. Her masculine counterpart is Tehuti, who is the male version of her with similar attributes. In other interpretations, however, Tehuti is paired with Seshat who is the goddess of measure and writing.

Several of her chief functions include the regulation of seasons and the stars along with stopping the world from going back into disorder. After these roles were well-established, she represented the spiritual weight of the heart of the deceased in the afterworld. Her feather is used to determine whether the soul of the departed rest in the heart. If so, the dead successfully ascends to paradise.

The impact of Maat is considered greatly significant in the lives of the living as well as of the dead. Kemetians (Egyptians) were expected to adhere to the truth and ethical morals in all aspects of their daily deeds to include God, family, community and nation. The principles of Maat were created to address the diverse populace with incompatible interests and complex needs in an evolving nation of Kemet. The development of Maat averted disorder and chaos, forming the essence of Kemetic laws.

As the principles of Maat continued to expand, they included additional dynamics of human life: harmony in the universe, relationship encounters, celestial activities, seasonal cycles, observations of religion, faith, good, and honesty. Kemetians committed to unity and wholeness of the universe. They achieved peace in the cosmos through ceremonial rituals and daily life. If the harmony of the cosmos was imbalanced, they would suffer the impact both individually and collectively as a state.

The law of Maat also covered traditions regarding change, impartiality, righteousness, and rhetorical questioning. During the Middle Kingdom, 2062 BCE – 1664 BCE, sacred writings declared, "I made every man like his fellow". According to Maat, those with riches were obligated to assist those who were less fortunate because it was wrong to exploit the have nots (Morenz, p. 273).

The ostrich feather is used in the crown of Maat; it personifies truth, harmony and justice. Africans outside of Kemet wore the ostrich feather as a sign of their highest devotion. In Ancient Kemet, however, the use of animal feathers was calculating and beyond appearance. They used them for references based on the characteristics and behavior of the animal. For example, the ostrich symbolizes truth in Kushite-Kemetic spiritual science.

Firstly, the importance of the ostrich is that it is exclusively from Africa. This meant to the Kushite-Kemetic people that "Truth" is only in Africa. They viewed their rivals in West Asia as the speakers of many untruths.

The second reason,the eyes of the ostrich are the largest of any land mammal in the world, making it ideal to represent truth. Their eyes, also, are bigger than its brain, which is why it is symbolic of truth. Thus, the ostrich's feather is a representation of what Maat sees.

In addition, the Kushite-Kemetic people saw the eyes as sacred "of the Supreme Being in His form as Ra". Since they exaggerated the size of their own eyes in their arts, the ostrich possessed a desirable attribute. Ra gave this sacred eye to Tehuti to help Heru conquer Setekh. This eye is seen as the chief observer of truth over book knowledge or information heard with the ear. The ostrich, therefore, became the consecrated animal as a symbol of Maat *(Karenga, p. 38).*

The third reason focuses on the endurance of the ostrich which is the fastest of any animal on land. In a short sprint, cheetahs are faster; however, the high speed and endurance of an ostrich surpass all other land animals. An ostrich can run 40 mph for more than an hour. The endurance and speed of an ostrich, thus, symbolize the Truth of Maat. Falsehood may win the short race, but only truth has the endurance to last forever!!!!

For these three divine reasons, our ancestors chose the ostrich as the representation of Maat. The myth that an ostrich buries his/her head in the sand to avoid immediate danger was a Roman myth, demonizing the African ostrich that signifies the Truth of Maat (Wikipedia, "Maat"). Our ancestors said, "Truth is only in Africa; truth is the ostrich feather of Ma'at".

This is a passage in the Instruction of Ptahhotep, the author of the world's first book. He presented Maat as follows:

"Maat is good and its worth is lasting.
It has not been disturbed since the day of its creator.
Whereas who transgresses its ordinances is punished.
It lies as a path in front even of him who knows nothing.
Wrongdoing has never yet brought its venture to port.
It is true that evil may gain wealth,
but the strength of truth is that it lasts;
A man can say: "It was the property of my father."

(Photo Credit, Daniel Laroche, Nile River Valley, Kemet)

32

As written on the Papyrus of Ani and sourced in The Book of the Dead (*pp. 97–96*), the 42 Laws of MAAT, also represented by the Ankh, declare:

1. I have not committed sin.
2. I have not committed robbery with violence.
3. I have not stolen.
4. I have not slain men and women.
5. I have not stolen grain.
6. I have not purloined offerings.
7. I have not stolen the property.
8. I have not uttered lies.
9. I have not carried away food.
10. I have not uttered curses.
11. I have not committed adultery;
12. I have made none to weep.
13. I have not eaten the heart (i.e. I have not grieved uselessly, or felt remorse).
14. I have not attacked any man.
15. I am not a man of deceit.
16. I have not stolen cultivated land.
17. I have not been an eavesdropper.
18. I have slandered no man.
19. I have not been angry without just cause.
20. have not debauched the wife of any man.
21. I have not debauched the wife of any man
22. I have not polluted myself.
23. I have terrorized none.
24. I have not transgressed the Law.
25. I have not been wroth.
26. I have not shut my ears to the words of truth.

27. I have not blasphemed.

28. I am not a man of violence.

29. I am not a stirrer-up of strife (or a disturber of the peace).

30. I have not acted (or judged) with undue haste.

31. I have not pried into matters.

32. I have not multiplied my words in speaking.

33. I have wronged none; I have done no evil.

34. I have not worked witchcraft against the King (or blasphemed against ....the King).

35. I have never stopped the flow of water.

36. I have never raised my voice (spoken arrogantly or in anger).

37. I have not cursed or blasphemed God.

38. I have not acted with evil rage.

39. I have not stolen the bread,

40. I have not carried away the khenfu cakes from the spirits of the dead.

41. I have not snatched away the bread of the child, nor treated with contempt the God of my city.

42. I have not slain the cattle.

Myth: Moral commandments originally came from the Bible.

Enlightenment: Moral Commandments existed for thousands of years before the Bible.

Facts: These 42 laws come from the Papyrus of Ani.

(Photo credit: Daniel Laroche, Papyrus of Ani, British Museum, England, UK)

Anubis is a jackal-headed Neter` (deity) who oversees the embalming process as well as escorts the deceased kings to the afterworld. The people of ancient Kemet followed the laws of MAAT. In order to pass into the afterworld and join Ausar, the dead must have a heart lighter than a feather. Anubis is seen weighing the heart of Ani to see if it is lighter than a feather for entrance into the afterlife.

In Proverbs 21 of the Bible, it states, "The king's heart is in the hand of the LORD; he directs it like a watercourse wherever he pleases. All a man's ways seem right to him, but the LORD weighs the heart. To do what is right and just is more acceptable to the LORD than sacrifice". This was an echo copy of Maat, determining if the heart of the dead is lighter than a feather to enter the afterworld. The spiritual principles of Maat were the measurement of justice instead of the "detailed legalistic exposition of rules". Maat was the values that shaped the backdrop for applying justice, truth and fairness. From the Fifth Dynasty (2510 - 2370 BCE) onward, the Priest of Maat, also so known as the vizier, oversaw the responsibility of justice. In later periods, judges adorned images of Maat.

Scholars and great thinkers in later centuries also began to include concepts from the Sebayt.

Sebayt is the ancient Egyptian term for a certain type of literature about the pharaohs (nst bity/kings). The word actually translates to mean "teachings" or "instructions". These teachings were formal and ethical writings about the "way of living truly" and were acknowledged as wisdom literature. These texts focused on social and professional disputes that transpired daily. They offered the fairest way to address disagreements, using the measurement of Maat. Strongly case-based, they served as practical guidance so that general and specific directions could be derived from them in resolving domestic and state conflicts (Lichtheim).

Facts: The Shabaka Stone describes how Ra (the Sun Neter) came about. Ra was the king of the deities and the father of all creation. Ra was the patron of the sun, heaven, kingship, power and light. Ra was not only the Neter who governed the actions of the sun, but also could be the physical sun.

According to the text on the Shabaka Stone as presented in Homer Smith's Man and His Gods, the world was brought into being by Ptah who is an ancient Kemetic deity, a co-creator and patron of architects and craftsmen. In the Memphis trinity described on the Shabaka Stone, the husband of Sekhmet and the father of Nefertem is Ra. Sometimes, Ra was considered the father of the sage Imhotep (p. 45). These words uttered from the Stone:

There took shape in the heart; there took shape on the tongue the form of Atum. For the very great one is Ptah, who gave [life] to all the gods and their Kas [soul] through this heart and through this tongue...For every word of the God came about through what the heart devised, and the tongue commanded.

Heru came into being in him; Tehuti came into being in him as Ptah. Power came into being in the heart and by the tongue and in all limbs, in accordance with the teaching that the heart is in all bodies and mouths of all Gods, all men, all flocks, all creeping things and of everything which lives... And so, it is said of Ptah: He who made all and brought the gods into being. From him everything came forth: foods, provisions, divine offerings, all good things... Thus Ptah was satisfied after he had made all things and all divine words

The writings on the Shabaka Stone can be interpreted to mean that divinity is no longer restricted to the Gods but dispersed by Ptah to all creatures across the world. The Memphite Theology presents a Neter who goes forth into the world and becomes an integral part of the bodies and souls of all human beings. Ptah's divinity identifies with and includes nature. The Stone further proclaims:

> *"Lo, he gave birth to the Gods.*
> *He made the towns.*
> *He established the nomes.*
> *He placed the Gods in their shrines.*
> *He settled their offerings.*
> *He established their shrines.*
> *He made their bodies according to their wishes.*
> *Thus, the Gods entered into their bodies,*
> *of every kind of wood, of every kind of stone,*
> *of every kind of clay,*
> *in every kind of thing that grows upon him,*
> *in which they came to be.*
> *Thus, all the gods and their Kas were gathered to him,*
> *content and united with the Lord of the Two Lands".*

Myth: The origin of creation comes from the Bible.

Enlightenment: The origin and stories of creation come from Africa thousands of years before the Bible.

Facts: African Priest and Inpw/Anubis (Lord of the Dead) is pouring water over the King, preparing the King for his journey through the afterlife. Water is pictorially symbolized as the Ankh. Seen below are details from the interior sarcophagus of Amenemipet, a priest of Amenohotep.

Temple of Amen

(Photo Credit: Bridgeman Images)

Myth: The Catholic Church started baptism and libation.

Enlightenment: Libations and pouring water in spiritual ceremonies started in Africa thousands of years before the Catholic Church was conceived.

Facts: Ausar, personified as a shrouded mummy, signifies his transformed state from life to dead. He holds a flail and short shepherd's crook insignia, associated with Kemetic kingship. He wears a long, braided beard emblematic of divinity. An uraeus is seen on the front of his tall crown with a spitting fire cobra as protection from his enemies. The horns of Ausar connect him with the sun God, who at days end, night time, appears as a ream-headed being (Alchin).

(Photo credit: Daniel Laroche MD, Metropolitan Museum, New York)

(Photo credit: Daniel Laroche MD, Metropolitan Museum, New York)

In ancient Kemetic spirituality, Auset was an extremely important Goddess whose influences advanced the thinking of the Greco-Roman society as well as modern-day Christianity. Referenced first in the Old Kingdom (2686 – 2181 BCE), Auset was a pivotal Goddess in the Ausar story. In this creation story, she breathed new life into the king, who was her husband, as well as her slain brother. Auset and her husband-king produced a son Heru in which she protects the king's heir. It is believed that Auset helped the departed enter the afterworld as she had done for her husband-king, Ausar. She was viewed as the divine mother of the pharaoh (nst/bityking), who was the father of Heru.

Auset's ability to heal extended to the common people. Originally, she was limited to sacred rituals and royal ceremonies but later became more visible in spiritual writings and funeral rites. She is depicted in art as a Neter who is adorned with a throne-like hieroglyph on her crown. Auset later was characterized with traits more commonly associated with Hathor during the New Kingdom (1550 – 1070 BCE). Thus, portrayals of Auset have been seen with her wearing the headdress of Hathor, which includes "a sun disk between the horns of a cow".

In the first millennium BCE, Auset and Ausar were the most worshipped Kemetic Neters. As popularity of the Ausar Story grew among the people of Kemet (Egypt), Auset absorbed qualities from other Neters. Thus, Kemetian ruling class along with its southern neighbor, Nubia, erected sacred temples, mostly honoring Isis, but Auset was not left out. The temple for Auset at Philae was a religious sanctuary for the people of Kemet and Nubia. The spiritual power of Auset was greater than that of all other deities. She was considered the protector of the kingdom from enemies, governor of the natural world and skies, and Goddess over fate itself (Pinch).

Myth: The Bible had the first trinity of Mary, Jesus and God.
Enlightenment: The trilogy of Ausar, Auset and Heru was the first trinity that predates the Bible by thousands of years.

Quoted from the Story of Ausar, Auset and Heru as told in the Muata Ashby:
> *Ausar was an early leader of Kush, and genius who developed the written word, agriculture, and theology. Armed with this knowledge, Ausar left Kush to spread his teachings along the Nile Valley and around the world.*

On his teaching travels, he met a beautiful Nubian woman named Auset, whom he married shortly thereafter. Auset remained in her homeland while her husband continued in his travels as a teacher.

Ausar gained fame and admiration throughout Kemet as a unifier, a man of order and virtue, and an exemplary scholar. This fame provoked the envy and hatred of his brother, Set.

As Ausar traveled across Kemet unifying the wild and scattered tribes into the world's first nation-state, his brother followed behind him like a harsh wind in an attempt to undo his brother's accomplishments. Set stirred up animosity among those who had come under Ausar's rule.

"Who is he that you should listen to Ausar?" Set would proclaim. "Let each man do as he pleases!"

Lawlessness exploded across the region, and the order that Ausar brought to Kemet began to deteriorate. Nevertheless, Set was not satisfied with the chaos that he wrought – he wanted his brother dead.

Set followed behind Ausar, caught up to him, and murdered him while he slept. He dismembered Ausar's body into 14 pieces and spread them across Kemet so that they could not be found.

When Auset learned of the murder of her husband, she fled into hiding and then went searching for the missing parts of her husband's body. She found every piece, except for Ausar's penis. It had been cast into the Nile and eaten by a crocodile.

She cleaned each piece of her husband's body, anointed it with oil, and wrapped him in linens. She grieved over her beloved, not only because he was murdered but because they hadn't consummated their marriage – Auset was still a virgin.

The spirit of Ausar heard her cries and visited her in the night. Nine months later, Auset gave birth to Heru. Heru, endowed with the spirit of his father, was given the mission of defeating his wicked uncle Set and restoring order to his father's kingdom on Earth as the rightful heir to a unified Kemet.

Heru grew up in hiding to prevent Set from discovering that Ausar had an anointed son, but all the while preached of his father's kingdom and preparing his disciples for the day of battle. The battle between the forces of Set, in the North, against the forces of Heru, in the South, was apocalyptic.

Once the battle was over, instead of killing his uncle Set, Heru bound him in chains and cast him into an abyss. At the moment of his victory, Heru was transformed into a falcon and was called up into heaven to stand before his father and give testament.

Ausar was well pleased, blessed him, and sent him back down to Earth to rule as the legitimate Pharaoh of a unified Kemet. Once Heru assumed his throne on Earth, Ausar was also able to be at rest and assumed his throne as the Lord of the Underworld.

To commemorate the victory of Heru, every temple and royal house carved a winged sun – the heru bedet – above its entrance. The heru bedet served as a reminder of the virtues of order and a warning against the dangers of greed and jealousy.

And that is the Story of Ausar, Aset and Heru!!!

"Judgment Scene" from the Book of the Dead of Hunefer, New Kingdom, 19th dynasty, ca. 129–80 BCE

(Photo credit: Daniel Laroche, British Museum, London, UK)

Nebet-het (Nephthys) is the sister of Auset and Ausar in addition to being the sister-consort of Set. Throughout Kemetic history, she was linked with funerary practices in the Old Kingdom. She was considered the "Lady with Wings" in which she guides the newly departed through the underworld and comforts the living relatives of the deceased. In some of the first portrayals, Nebet-het appears in "funerary literature" where she sails in a "night boat" in the underworld. She meets the spirit of the dead king and leads him into the "Lightland". Her hair metaphorically represents the pieces of cloth wrapping the body of the king (El-Shahawy, p. 106).

Facts: One of the most noteworthy Kemetic (Egyptian) Neters was Heru, who had several important functions. His most famous role was existing as the Neter of kingship and the great sky. He has been revered from pre-historic Kemetic times until the present. His symbolic representation often was the falcon. The falcon is considered the fastest fowl on earth with vision, seeing for miles away. Here, Heru wears the crowns of both upper Kemet and lower Kemet (Redford & Meltzer, pp. 164 – 168).

Heru at Temple of Edfu

(Photo credit: Daniel Laroche, Kemet)

Myth: The people of Ancient Kemet worshiped animals.

Enlightenment: The people of Kemet had a great deal of symbolism such as the falcon, which is the fastest bird that can fly over two hundred miles per hour and has keen sight, seeing for over two miles and can fly above a storm.

Facts: Building in Ancient Kemet using simple tools, techniques and skillful administration, the people of ancient Kemet were able to build structures that appear daunting even to today's construction standards. Stone and mud brick were the most used building materials and in abundant supply throughout the area. Stone was used primarily for tombs and temples that were intended to last for eternity. Mud brick, on the other hand, often was used for more complex buildings such as houses and palaces. Because timber suitable for construction was in short supply in the Nile Valley, the people of Kemet became very adept at using enormous slabs of stone for rafters, architraves, roofing, and columns.

The interior and exterior surfaces of the buildings were often decorated with carved scenes and hieroglyphic inscriptions. Designs were carved with metal chisels in either raised or sunken reliefs; tiles, plaster and paint were used to further embellish surfaces. The initiation of a monumental building project was often accompanied by elaborate rituals that were thought to purify the site and to commemorate the pharaoh who commissioned the structure. The tombs subsequently became more elaborate, educational, and secure to prevent theft (Mark, "Ancient Egyptian Architecture").

King Djoser

Notice His Black Braided Locks

(Photo credit: Daniel Laroche, Cairo Museum, Kemet)

King Djoser

(Photo credit: Daniel Laroche, Cairo Museum, Kemet)

Currently housed in the Egyptian Museum in Cairo, the decorated limestone of Djoser is the most ancient, life-sized Egyptian statue known in the world.

Also spelled as Djeser or Zoser, Djoser was an ancient Kemetic (Egyptian) pharaoh (nst bity/king) of the Third Dynasty during the Old Kingdom. Djoser was the son of Queen Nimaathap and King Khasekhemwy. His most noted contribution was his step pyramid, which is several mastaba (tombs) layered over one another. This form of pyramid building eventually set the standard for constructing pyramid tombs throughout the later Old Kingdom. One contemporary of king Djoser was his high official Vizier Tjaty, who oversaw all stone work in the royal shipyard (Britannica, "Djoser".)

Myth: Africans contributed nothing to architecture.

Enlightenment: Africans were the originators of architecture and highly skilled in mathematics and science.

Imohotep Statute

(Photo credit: Daniel Laroche MD, Cairo Museum, Kemet)

Facts: Imhotep oversaw stone building projects such as the tombs of King Djoser and King Sekhemkhet. Djoser was buried in his famous step pyramid at Saqqara. This pyramid was originally built as a nearly square mastaba (tomb), but then five further mastabas were literally piled one upon another, each smaller than the previous one. The monument became Egypt's first step pyramid. The high priest, Imhotep, was the supervisor of the building constructions of this pyramid (Britannica, "Imhotep").

He was a skilled architect who designed the step pyramid of (Mrkhut) Djoser and believed to be the first stone structure in human history. At Heliopolis, he was the high priest of the sun Neter Ra. He became recognized as a mastermind of math and science, exemplified in his talents as an architect and physician.

Although Djehuty/Thoth is the actual Kemetic Neter of mathematics, architecture as well as medicine, Imhotep was eventually heightened to the same prominence. His supporters and patrons ceased in upholding him as a "guardian" deity but help to elevate his status to a "true" god. He is one of two of non-regal blood who continues to be glorified into the present day. In fact, Imhotep along with Amenhotep, son of Hapu, are the only two to receive such reverence. In city of Thebes (Ancient Kemet), Amenhotep is deified as a mastermind architect in which temples are dedicated to him. Also, the Greeks like to compare their Askleois to Imhotep because of the similarities in construction design and medicine (Hurry).

Actualized frequently, the libation to Imhotep and the statues of Imhotep were illustrated on papyri text until the Late Period (664 – 332 BCE). Imhotep was known for his compelling writings of wisdom. He scribed many maxims (revelations) that shape modern day thinking such as "Eat, drink and be merry for tomorrow we shall all die". He also is considered the "Father of Medicine". He inscribed several important medical regiments that are still used in modern medicine. As a skilled anatomist, who used plants to heal the sick, Imhotep cured 200 diseases and performed many medical and dental surgeries (Britannica, "Imhotep").

The Coffin of Imhotep

(Photo credit: Daniel Laroche MD, Imhotep Museum, Cairo, Kemet)

Myth: Africans contributed nothing to medicine.

Enlightenment: Africans were the founders of medicine, science and architecture.

The Step Pyramid at Saqqara Designed by Imhotep

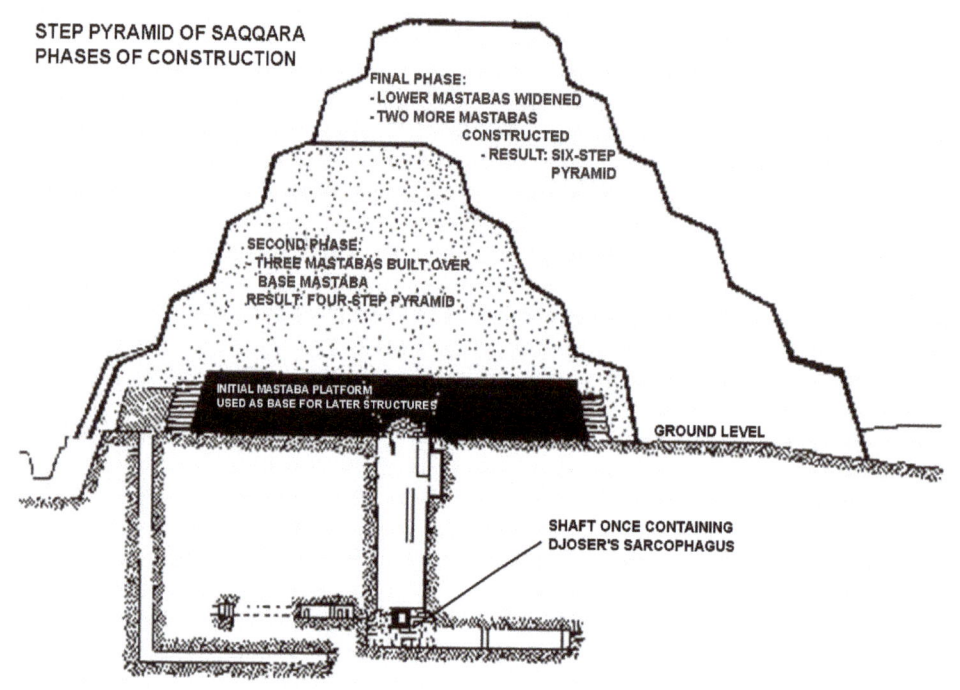

**STEP PYRAMID OF SAQQARA
PHASES OF CONSTRUCTION**

FINAL PHASE:
- LOWER MASTABAS WIDENED
- TWO MORE MASTABAS CONSTRUCTED
- RESULT: SIX-STEP PYRAMID

SECOND PHASE:
- THREE MASTABAS BUILT OVER BASE MASTABA
- RESULT: FOUR-STEP PYRAMID

INITIAL MASTABA PLATFORM USED AS BASE FOR LATER STRUCTURES

GROUND LEVEL

SHAFT ONCE CONTAINING DJOSER'S SARCOPHAGUS

Pyramid of Djoser

(Photo credit: Daniel Laroche, Saqqara, Kemet)

52

The Step Pyramid was built during the reign of the Third Dynasty of King Djoser (2683 – 2686 BCE). It was the first ever attempted of a colossal stone structure in history. Previously, ancient Kemetic, royal tombs consisted of a single mastaba made of mudbrick, but thanks to the genius of the architect Imhotep, a new type of tomb was developed that consisted of six mastabas on top of one another.

The pyramid has two entrances. The first one is on the north side and is the original entrance that dates to the Third Dynasty. The burial chamber lies at the end of a series of corridors, five floors down. Inside, it is a massive pink granite, burial vault, sized at 5.35 meters in length, 3.47 meters in width and 4.73 meters in height. It consists of 32 granite blocks and weighs a total of 176 tons.

The second entrance on the south side of the pyramid was made around two thousand years later, when the kings of the Twenty-Sixth Dynasty (525 – 664 BCE) took care of the monuments after their illustrious predecessors. Naturally, Djoser was one of the revered kings of the past, so the ruling kingdom declared measures to renovate his pyramid. This is evidenced by the stone columns, reinforcing the ceiling of the passages from the pyramid's entrance, and the wooden beams used to support the central shaft's ceiling. The granite burial vault lies at the bottom of the shaft, which is 7x7 meters and 28 meters deep (Kinnaer, "Funerary-complex").

Facts: Burials of Predynastic bodies and material for the afterlife were buried in a sand pit or rock pit, but robbers stole the materials (Dorman & Faulkner).

(Photo credit: Daniel Laroche MD, Nubian Museum, Aswan)

Mummies were then placed beneath the pyramids to preserve them.

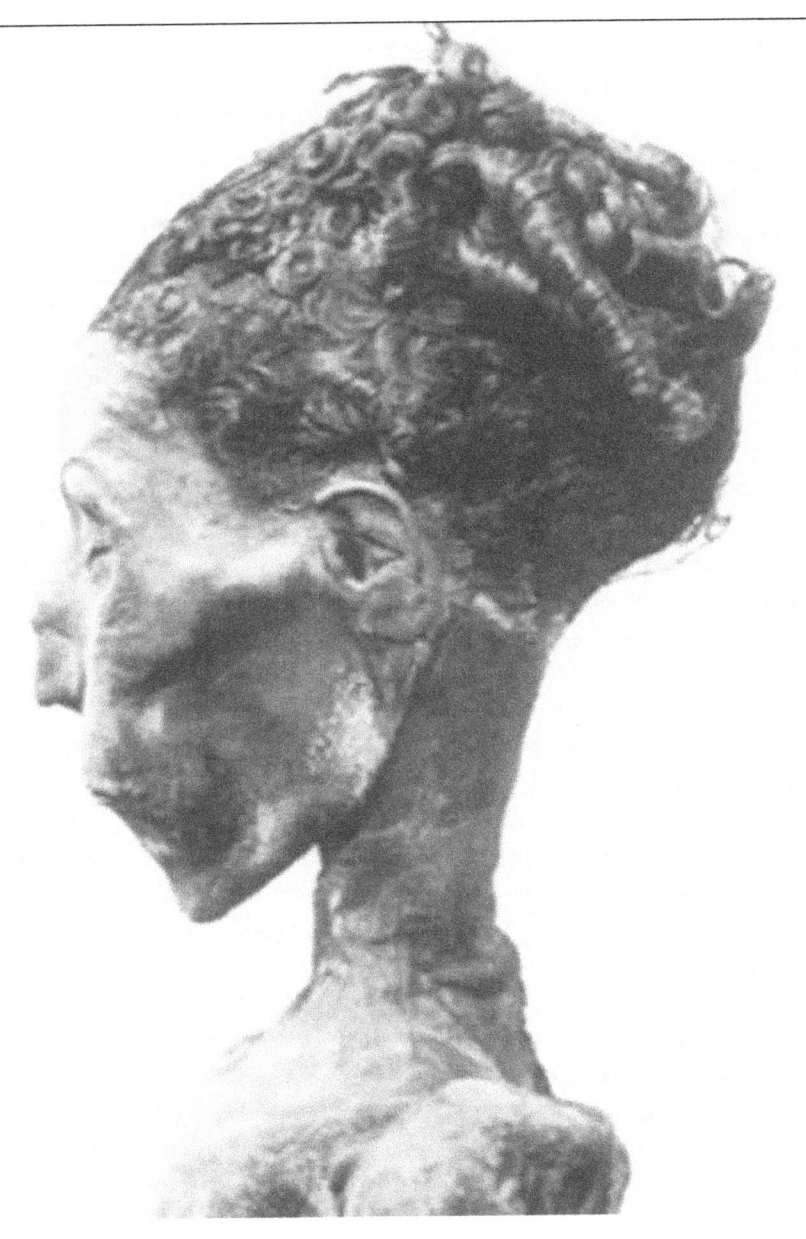

(Photo credits: Asa Hilliard, http://www.narmer.pl/listy/list_en.htm)

The mummy of Ria (Figs 34 and 35)

(Photo credits: Asa Hilliard, http://www.narmer.pl/groby/db320_en.htm)

56

(Mummy of Queen Tiye, https://thebanmappingproject.com/glossary/tiye)

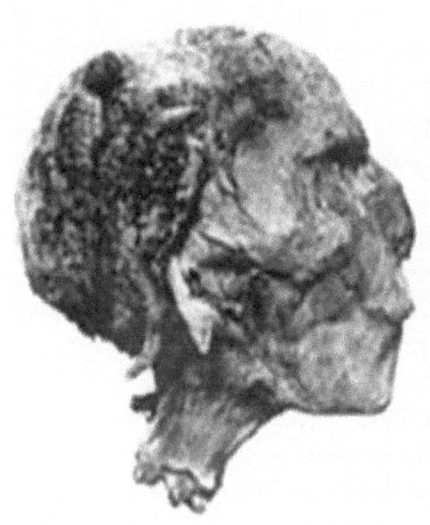

(Photo credit: Asa Hilliard, http://www.narmer.pl/groby/db320_en.htm)

Myth: Ancient Kemetians were white people, so whites were shrouded as mummies.

Enlightenment: Melanin testing of the mummies confirmed Ancient Kemetic mummies were African and Nubian (Black).

Serdab at the Step Pyramid

The precise definition of a serdab means "cold water" and later became the primary word in the Arabic language for cellar. In Ancient Kemet, a serdab is a burial chamber for the Ka (soul) statue of the newly departed.

The Serdab was a sealed off room in a tomb in which a statue of the deceased was placed. The statues were vessels that the soul could inhabit. Djoser's serdab is located on the north side of the Step Pyramid in front of an open court dedicated to him. A statue depicting the king wearing the Sed Festival robe was discovered inside. Just as the Step Pyramid is the oldest ancient Egyptian, monumental stone structure, it is the first large stone statue. The original is currently in the Egyptian Museum.

Two holes made through the wall directly facing the king's gaze allowed the king to peer through and see the rituals and festivals taking place in the court before him. These holes also allowed the king to look north, the cardinal point toward which his entire pyramid complex is oriented. This is the location of the circumpolar stars in the northern sky and his ancestors, whom he hoped to join. These stars never set below the horizon, which was seen as a sign of immortality. Djoser, thus, was poised to join his forefathers in everlasting life (Bard).

(Photo credit: Daniel Laroche MD, Saqqara, Kemet)

Facts: Hesy-Ra was the world's first dentist.

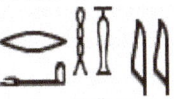

(Photo credit: Daniel Laroche MD, Cairo Museum, Cairo, Kemet)

(Photo credit: Daniel Laroche MD, Cairo Museum, Cairo, Kemet)

60

(Photo credit: Daniel Laroche MD, Cairo Museum, Cairo, Kemet)

61

(Photo credit: Daniel Laroche MD, Cairo Museum, Cairo, Kemet)

Also spelled Hesy-Re or Hesire, Hesy-Ra was a high official in ancient Kemet during the early Third Dynasty. He held the title of Wer-ibeḥ-senjw, which means either "Great one of the ivory cutters" or "Great one of the dentists", making him the earliest named dentist.

His tomb is famously known for its luxuriously-decorated panels and painted adornment. On the cedar wood panels, the stages of his life are detailed. The panels closest to the entrance display him as a young man at the beginning of his career. The ones closer to the remembrance chapel depict Hesy-Ra as a middle-aged professional at the peak of his livelihood. Finally, the panels nearest the remembrance chapel, he is portrayed in his old age, "sitting on an offering table and being stuffed in a tight gown". The artist of the panels was able to capture authentic facial expressions of his aging. The face of Hesy-Ra transforms from smooth to saggy and wrinkled in each respective stage of his life. (John F. Nunn: Ancient Egyptian Medicine. Oklahoma Press, Normal 2002, ISBN 0-8061-3504-2, page 124).

Myth: Africans contributed nothing to dentistry.

Facts: Africans invented dentistry and Hesy-Ra was the first one.

Pyramid of Unas with Step Pyramid in Background

(Photo credit: Daniel Laroche MD, Saqqara, Kemet)

Also known as, "Beautiful are the places of Unas", the Pyramid of Unas was erected for the Kemetic king (pharaoh) Unas in the 24th century BCE during the Fifth Dynasty. It was built between the complexes of Sekhemket and Djoser in North Saqqara. Anchored to the valley temple at a nearby lake, a long causeway was constructed to provide access to the pyramid site. With a smooth outside texture, the Pyramid of Unas is the smallest of the Old Kingdom pyramids but has great significance because of the texts that were discovered there (Wikipedia, "Pyramid of Unas").

Inscribed for the first time in the pyramid of Unas, the tradition of funerary texts carried on in the pyramids of subsequent rulers. This style of funeral ritual was performed through the end of the Old Kingdom into the Middle Kingdom up until the Coffin Texts. The Coffin Texts formed the basis of the Pert em Heru, also known as The Book of the Dead since it was found near dead mummies.

The 283 readings in the pyramid of Unas constitute the oldest and best-preserved text of spiritual writing from the Old Kingdom. Their function was to guide the ruler through eternal life and ensure his continued survival, even if the kingdom ceased to function. In the circumstance of Unas, the culture may have survived the turbulent First Intermediate Period and up until the Twelfth or Thirteenth Dynasty during the Middle Kingdom.

The earliest Kemetic funerary texts are called Pyramid Texts, which date back as far as 2400 – 2300 BCE in the late Old Kingdom. They are the oldest known collection of Kemetic spiritual writings. From the end of the Fifth Dynasty and throughout the Sixth Dynasty of the Old Kingdom into the Eighth Dynasty of the First Intermediate Period, inscriptions of the texts were carved on the walls and coffins (sarcophagi) of the pyramids at Saqqara.

Dissimilar to the later Pert Em Heru and Coffin Texts, Pyramid Texts were only for the ruling class pharaohs and did not contain illustrated details. The frequency and application of Pyramid Texts switched during the Old, Middle and New Kingdoms of Ancient Kemet (Egypt). During the Old Kingdom between 2686 and 2181 BCE and Middle Kingdom between 2055 and 1650 BCE, Pyramid Texts also were found in the pyramids of pharaohs as well as queens such as Wedjebten, Neith and Iput (Wikipedia, "Pyramid Texts").

Pyramid of Unas

(Photo credit: Courtesy of Photographer *Rune Nyord*)

After death, the pharaoh first must rise from his mastaba (tomb). Utterance 373 describes:

Oho! Oho! Rise up, O Teti!
Take your head, collect your bones,
Gather your limbs, shake the earth from your flesh!
Take your bread that rots not, your beer that sours not,
Stand at the gates that bar the common people!
The gatekeeper comes out to you, he grasps your hand,
Takes you into heaven, to your father Geb.
He rejoices at your coming, gives you his hands,
Kisses you, caresses you,
Sets you before the spirits, the imperishable stars...
The hidden ones worship you,
The great ones surround you,
The watchers wait on you,
Barley is threshed for you,
Emmer is reaped for you,
Your monthly feasts are made with it,
Your half-month feasts are made with it,
As ordered done for you by Geb, your father,
Rise up, O Teti, you shall not die!

The text then describes several ways for the pharaoh to reach the heavens, one of which is by climbing a ladder. In utterance 304, the king says:

Hail, daughter of Anubis, above the hatches of heaven,
Comrade of Thoth, above the ladder's rails,
Open Unas's path, let Unas pass!

Another way is by ferry. If the boatman refuses to take him, the king has other plans:

If you fail to ferry Unas,
He will leap and sit on the wing of Thoth,
Then he will ferry Unas to that side!

In the words of the people of Ancient Kemet, an oral tradition states:
"WE COME FROM THE BEGINNING OF THE NILE WHERE THE GOD HAPI DWELLS, AT THE FOOTHILLS OF THE MOUNTAINS OF THE MOON".

Where is the beginning of the Nile?

"The Nile River flows from SOUTH to NORTH through eastern Africa. It begins in the rivers that flow into Lake Victoria (located in modern-day Uganda, Tanzania, and Kenya), and empties into the Mediterranean Sea more than 6,600 kilometers (4,100 miles) to the north, making it one of the longest rivers in the world. In addition to Egypt, the Nile runs through or along the border of 10 other African countries, namely, Burundi, Tanzania, Rwanda, the Democratic Republic of the Congo, Kenya, Uganda, Sudan, Ethiopia, and South Sudan"

Considered "Mountains of the Moon, the Rwenzori Mountain borders the Democratic Republic of the Congo and Uganda. Wallis Budge in his book, Budge's Egypt: A Classical 19th-Century Travel Guide, remarks: "There are many things in the manners and customs of the historic people of Kemet that suggest…the original home of their pre-historic ancestors was a country in the neighborhood of Uganda and Punt".

Nile River in Kemet

(Photo credit: Getty Images, zhouyousifang stock,
https://www.history.com/news/ancient-egypt-nile-river)

Also included in the Pyramid Text is the Family Tree of the Great Ennead, Heliopolitan Ennead. The Ennead was a group of nine deities in Kemetic spirituality: the sun god Atum; his children Shu and Tefnut; their children Geb and Nut; and their children Osiris (Ausar), Isis (Auset), Set, and Nephthys. The Ennead sometimes includes the son of Osiris (Ausar), Isis (Auset), and Horus (Heru).

The Pyramid Text also documents the Family Tree of the Heliopolitan Ennead.

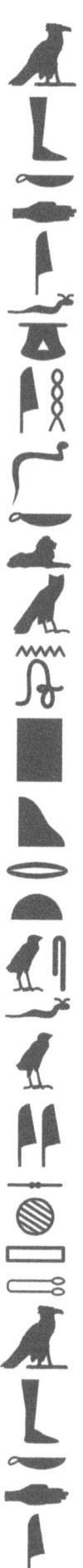

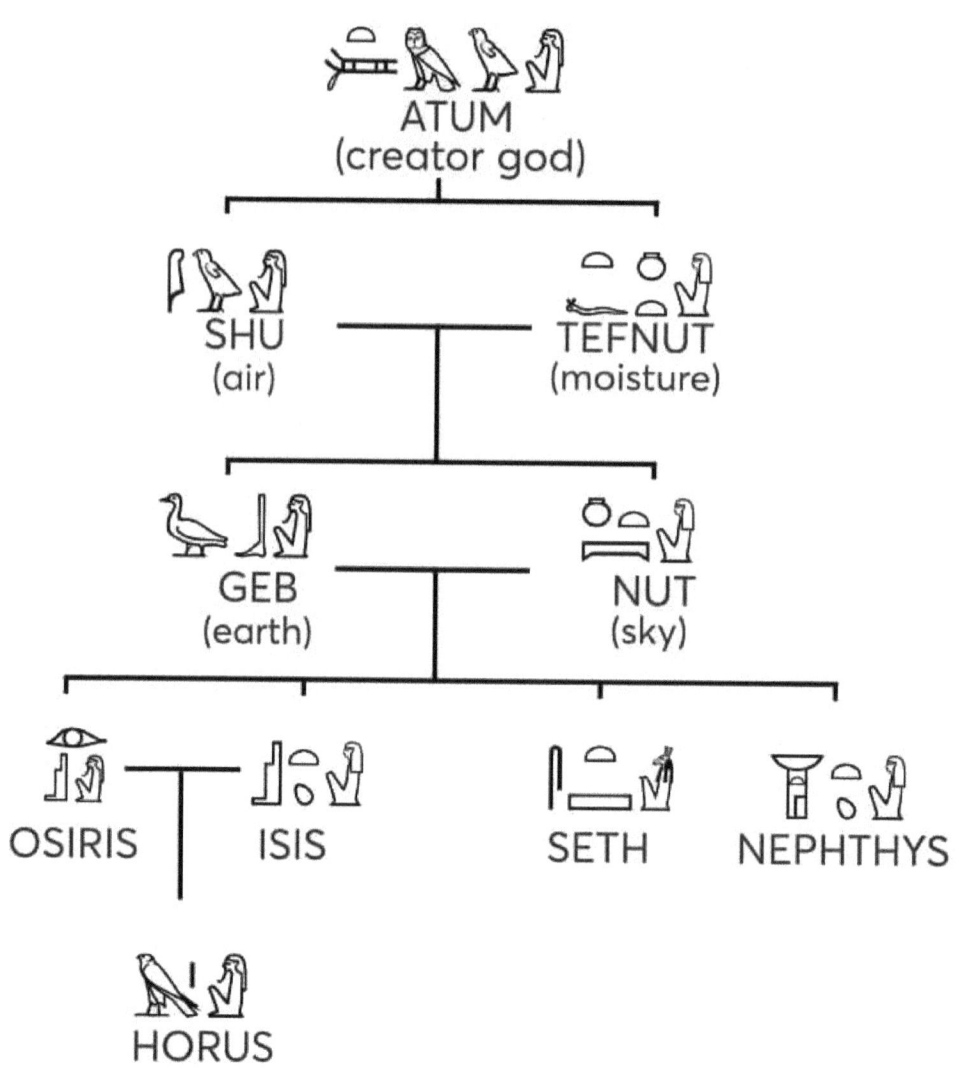

ATUM
(creator god)

SHU (air) — TEFNUT (moisture)

GEB (earth) — NUT (sky)

OSIRIS — ISIS   SETH   NEPHTHYS

HORUS

(Photo source: https://www.glencairnmuseum.org/newsletter/2021/7/13/ancient-egyptian-creation-myths-from-watery-chaos-to-cosmic-egg)

Myth: Ancient Africans did not maintain a written language.

Enlightenment: Africans invented spirituality and writing.

Fact: Sneferu is the father of Khufu.

Old Kingdom Dynasty 4

(Photo credit: Daniel Laroche, Cairo Museum, Kemet)

Snefru: 2613-2498

(Photo credit: Metesger books, Cairo Museum-Snefru stela from Dahshur)

Sneferu, also spelled Snefru or Snofru, means that the God of Maat has made him perfect or "He [Horus] has perfected me [Sneferu]". During the Old Kingdom, Sneferu formed the Fourth Dynasty of Kemet in which he reigned for nearly 24 years from 2613 to 2589 BCE, according to The Oxford History of Ancient Egypt. He was an important innovator of pyramid design and construction during his reign. He erected a minimum of three pyramids that still stand to this day. The dates calculating the kingship of Sneferu are based on a discovered inscription at the Red Pyramid of Dahshur and included a 24th cattle count, which indicates at least 24 full years. Presently, this calculation is considered an underestimate, since his highest-known date is a 24-year Turin Canon figure. He ruled approximately three years after the dates of the cattle count. The 10th, 13th and 18th counts are illustrated at his Medium Pyramid, suggesting Sneferu reined Kemet for at least 27 complete years (Wikipedia, "Sneferu").

The Palermo Stone is one of seven surviving, upright stone pieces known as the Royal Annals in the Old Kingdom of Ancient Kemet (Egypt). The Stone highlights important events in each year of the kings' rule. The stele (upright stone) listed the pharaohs (kings) of Egypt from the First Dynasty (3150 – 2890 BCE) to the early share of the Fifth Dynasty (2392 – 2283 BCE) and probably made available thereafter. The Palermo Stone is housed at the Regional Archeological Museum, Antonio Salinas in Palermo, Italy, where its name was derived.

Rectos or sectioned segments divide up the Palermo Stone. Recto six at the bottom of the fragment illustrates the year of the seventh count of Sneferu. Further, recto seven on the following row shows the year of the eighth cattle count of Sneferu. The most intact column about Sneferu is in recto five. It reveals specific years and events during his reign but does not comment on the previous year (the sixth). Historically, Egyptologists account for only a few years of Sneferu's reign: the 2nd, 7th, 8th, 12th, 13th, 14th, 15th, 16th, 17th, 18th, 23rd, and 24th before considering

70

the years following the cattle count. During his kingship, the cattle count was inconsistent and not always performed biannually. The census dates exposed more dates without cattle counting compared to dates with cattle calculations. Thus, the unknown column must date to the year preceding the sixth cattle count, and Sneferu probably ruled a minimum of 28 or 30 years but no greater than 48 years. This estimate certainly would have allotted the necessary time for Sneferu to plan, design and oversee the construction of three pyramids (Wikipedia, "Palermo Stone").

Palermo Stone

(Photo credit: https://archive.org/stream/abhandlungenderk1902kn/#page/n526/mode/1up)

Sneferu Name from the Temple of Abydos, King List

(Photo credit: Daniel Laroche, Temple of Abydos, Kemet)

Three of the most eminent pyramids (mrkhut) in Dahhshur are the Bent Pyramid, the Red Pyramid, and the Meidum pyramid. King Sneferu probably commissioned the design and building of the three. Under his rule, the planning and construction of pyramids drastically evolved and later influenced Khufu's Great Pyramid, which continues to represent the apex of Ancient Kemet (Egypt) as one of the "Seven Wonders" of the world.

The innovations in pyramid (mrkhut) design and construction of King Sneferu are heavily visible in his implementation of the Meidum monument. Some scholars disclaim King Sneferu as the mastermind of the Meidum pyramid but crediting King Huni as the originator of it. Despite the unfounded research in favor of either pharaoh (nst/bity king), as a remarkable illustration, the Meidum monument reflects innovative ideology and engineering around the burial site of King Sneferu.

The focus of detail includes enormous stone construction as the physical testimony, used to transition from the stepped pyramid to the "true" pyramid formation. Archaeological examinations of the pyramid indicate the original plan was conceived as a seven-stepped pyramid, similar to the Djoser monument at Saqqara. In later adjustments, the designer-manager included other platforms to add such features as limestone facing for smoothness and angled finishes for a more authentic pyramid. The Meidum pyramid has two underground chambers, a descending northern passage and a burial vault. The design of the Meidum pyramid mostly adheres to traditional standards of previous tombs. For example, the burial room is situated directly within the main body near the ground level instead of being underneath the grand stone structure (Wikipedia, "Meidum").

Photo credit: Commons by Leoboudv using CommonsHelper)

73

The Bent Pyramid, also acknowledged as the Rhomboidal or Blunted Pyramid, possesses greater architectural evolution than the Meidum Pyramid. As in most pyramids, angles are significant. In the Bent Pyramid, the incline goes from 55° to approximately 43° in the upper levels. The initial pyramid planning probably did not account for this variation but was modified during development because of insecure accretion layers. To stabilize it, the top layers were laid horizontally thereby abandoning the step-pyramid approach.

The internal compartments of the Bent Pyramid also confirm other advancements in pyramid design. The two entryways of the pyramid include a doorway from the north and another from the west. Distinguished by intricate "diagonal portcullis systems" and corbel walls, the subterranean chambers are massive in size, and the entire monument measures at 50 million cubic feet. The Bent Pyramid is considered the largest pyramid built to date. Revealing more innovations, the adjacent structure of Sneferu's Bent Pyramid went against the convention of previous built pyramids in which the passageway descends northward. The doorway of the Bent monument, however, ascends westward.

Since 1965 the Bent Pyramid had been closed for tourism. In July 2019, Egyptian heads of state decided to reopen the pyramid to the public. Tourists can experience two 4,600-year-old chambers and journey through a narrow 79-meter tunnel near the northern entryway. Also, during the tour, tourists for the first time can access it since excavated in 1956. At 18-meters high, the "side pyramid" probably was constructed for the wife of King Sneferu (Wikipedia, "Bent Pyramid).

(Photo credit: Courtesy of Neithsabes)

The Red Pyramid of Sneferu, First True Pyramid

(Photo credit: Courtesy of Hajor)

Since the Red Pyramid was the last monument of King Sneferu, expectations are high for the most significant architectural improvements and modifications. The main body of the structure includes the burial vaults and rooms; however, no ascending hallway, diagonal portcullis, or western entryway —not even the remains of King Sneferu— were found during the excavation. His coffin and mummified corpse possibly are hidden in his secret last configuration.

Nevertheless, the architectural evolution of King Sneferu paved the way for later pyramid designers and builders. The first pharaoh (king) of the Fourth Dynasty established a precedent for his successors to surpass. The Great Pyramid of King Khufu far exceeds the benchmarks of King Sneferu in pyramid construction. As concepts in pyramid architecture evolved, the size of pyramids in Ancient Kemet (Egypt) decreased in dimension. The Pyramid of Menkaure, for example, is a mere fraction of the size of earlier pyramids. Perhaps, the rise of devotion to the sun Neter Ra directly and the decline in worshipping the pharaoh (king) influenced the shift in pyramid size (Wikipedia, "Menkaure").

Westcar Papyrus

(Photo credit: Photographer Відомості про дозвіл)

Westcar Papyrus is on display in the Ägyptisches Museum in Berlin. It tells the story of the turquoise pendant, which is another story seen in Exodus in the Bible. In the Westcar Papyrus, the son of Khufu, Bauefre tells the third story:

"They are set during the reign of Sneferu. They speak of the time when the king, feeling very bored. On the advice of his chief lector priest, Djadjamankh, king goes for a sail, along with twenty attractive young women. One of the girls drops a turquoise fish pendant in the water and is so upset by its loss that even the promise of a replacement from the royal treasury does not cheer her up. Djadjamankh then causes the water to fold over on itself so that the amulet can be retrieved". Moses parting the sea echoes what the chief priest performed. The Westcar Papyrus existed over 1500 years prior to the Bible. In full translation, the story begins:

Then Bauefre stood up to speak, and said: "I will let your majesty hear a wonder which happened in the time of your forefather Sneferu, justified, and is something that the chief lector priest Djadjamankh did". Then he told the story of the green jewel. Did.

…For days things have not happened. [Snefru went through] every room of the palace to seek distraction for himself but he couldn't find any. The he said, "go and bring me the chief lector priest and book scribe Djadjamankh" and he was brought to him immediately. Then his majesty said to him "I have gone through every room of the palace to find distraction for myself but I couldn't find any."

Then Djadjamankh said to him "Oh, may your Majesty go to the lake of the palace and man a ship with all beautiful women from inside your palace. The heart of your majesty will be cheered by seeing them row a trip back and forth and seeing the beautiful reeds of your lake and seeing its beautiful fields and water banks. Your heart will be gladdened by this so I will arrange a rowing trip."

Let there be brought to me twenty oars of ebony plated with gold, their handles of sandalwood plated with electrum. Let there be brought to me twenty women with beautiful bodies, well developed breasts, who have braided, and who have not yet given birth. And let me be brought to me twenty nets and give these nets to these women after their clothes have been taken off". All was done as his majesty commanded. Then they rowed back and forth and the heart of his majesty was gladdened by seeing them row.

Then one woman who was at the stroke oar got entangled in her braids and a fish pendant of real turquoise fell in the water. Then she became still, without rowing and her side became still, and his majesty said "can you not row?" and they said "our stroke has become still without rowing" and his majesty said to her "why are you not rowing?" and she said "this fish pendant of real turquoise has fallen into the water" then [he said] to [her] "it shall be replaced" and she said to him "I prefer the real one to a substitute" and then his majesty said "go and bring me the chief lector priest Djadjamankh" and he was brought immediately.

Then the chief lector priest Djadjamankh spoke a spell and put one side of the water of the lake on top of the other and found the fish pendant lying on a shard. He fetched it and gave it to its owner. Now the water was twelve cubits in the middle, and it ended up being twenty-four cubits after being folded up. Then he spoke a spell and the parts of the water of the lake returned to their positions. His majesty spent a day of celebration with the entire royal household and at the end he rewarded the chief lector priest Djadjamankh with every good thing.

Behold a wonder that happened in the time of your forefather, the King of Upper and Lower Egypt Sneferu, which is something the chief lector priest and book scribe Djadjamankh did.

Then his majesty the King of Upper and Lower Egypt Khufu said "let an offering be made of a thousand loaves of bread, a hundred jars of beer, one ox and two balls of incense to the King of Upper and Lower Egypt Senefru, justified, and let there be given one cake, one jug of beer, a large portion of meat and one ball of incense to the chief lector priest and book scribe Djadjamankh, as I have seen an example of his learning". One did as everything as his majesty had ordered.

(Photo credit: Olaf Tausch, Cairo Museum, Kemet)

Khnum Khufu, more commonly referred by his last name, was a pharaoh of Ancient Kemet (Egypt), and the Ancient Greek invaders renamed him Cheops. As the second king of the Fourth Dynasty in the first portion of the Old Kingdom, 26th century BCE, Khufu was the son of Sneferu and succeeded his father as monarch (2609 – 2584 BCE). Evidence suggests that Khufu commissioned the Great Pyramid of Giza (considered one of the "Seven Wonder of the Ancient World"). Many researchers contest this general belief because the reign of Khufu was not well documented. Nevertheless, discovered in temple ruins at Abydos in 1903 was a well-preserved 3 inch-tall, ivory figurine of King Khufu. The other statues and relics were badly fragmented in pieces, and his building structures still not found. The majority of information about Khufu comes from writings in his Necropolis at the Pyramid of Giza. Long after the death of Khufu, Ancient Kemetic scribers and Greek historians documented information on Khufu near 300 BCE (Wikipedia, "Khufu").

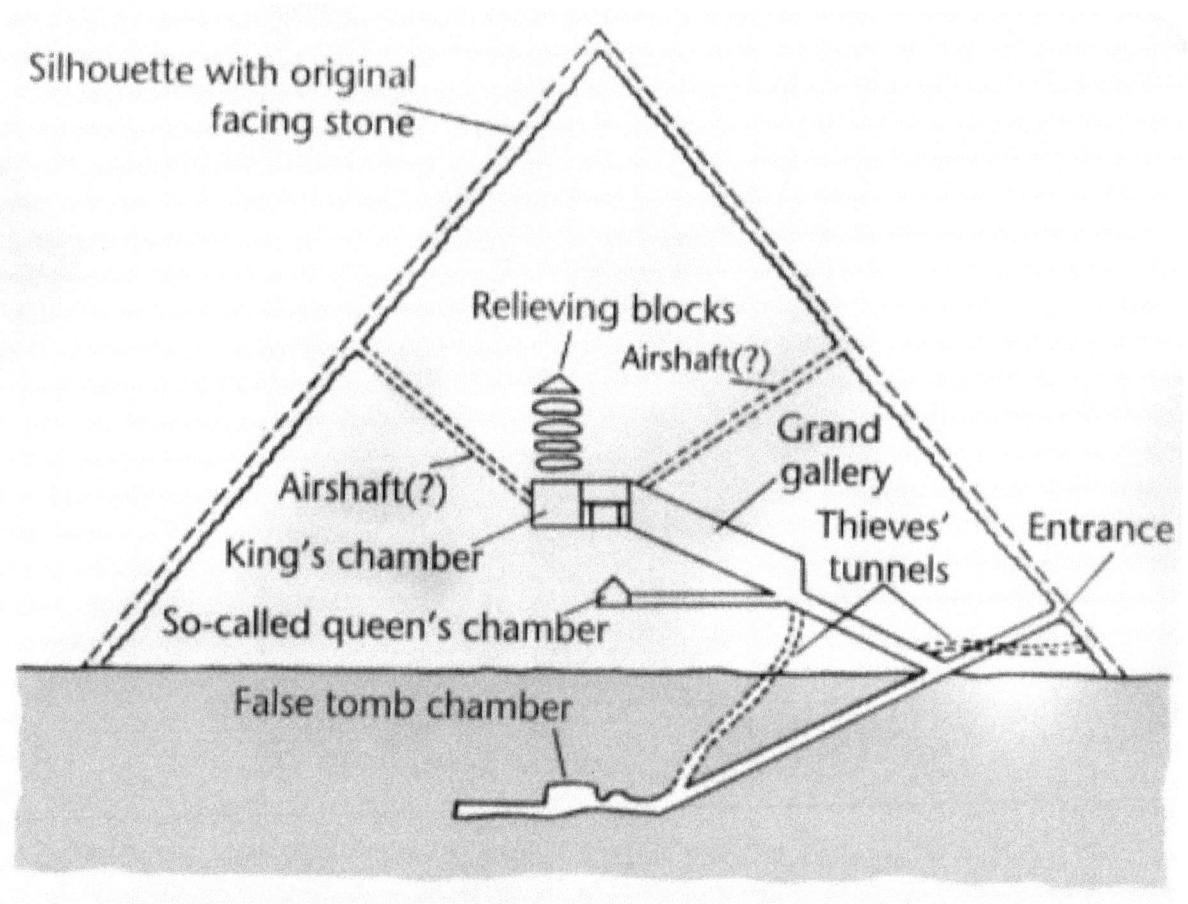

Section of the Great Pyramid of Khufu, Giza.

(Drawing credit: icrazeworld.wordpress.com)

Shen Text of Khufu

The Shen (an oval with a line at one end tangent to it, indicating that the text enclosed is a royal name) surrounding the name of King Khufu fashions the appearance of a rope. During his time, the actual personification of the pharaoh and the characteristics of his name did not always match with one another. The titulary was only on the Shen and believed the personal name of the pharaoh (Wikiwand, "Khufu").

(Photo credit: Windowsoftheworld.net)

(photo credit: https://mablculveq.blogspot.com/2021/06/ancient-egypt-pharaoh-khufu.html)

Khufu   Pyramid

(photo credit: Daniel Laroche)

Inside the Pyramid of Giza

(Photo credit: National Geographic general collection)

Myth: Aliens built the pyramids.

Enlightenment: Four generations of African families built the Pyramids of Giza.

Facts: Many ancient African buildings were built around the astronomy observed.

Sopdet

As the brightest star in the sky, Sirius, whose heliacal appearance intensifies, was the basis for the Solar Kemetic calendar. In Ancient Kemet, the star of Orion rose before Sirius and was regarded as a Neter called Sah. Sah was closely linked with Sopdet, the Neter who personified Sirius. The god Sopdu is said to be the son of Sah and Sopdet. Sah is syncretized with Osiris while Sopdet is syncretized with Osiris' mythological wife, Isis. In Pyramid Texts, from the 24th and 23rd centuries BCE, Sah is one of many Neters whose form the dead pharaoh can take in the afterlife (Shaltout, pp. 273 – 298).

Sopdet Seen with a Star above Her Head

(Photo credit: Daniel Laroche, Temple of Dendera, Kemet)

Orion's Belt or the Belt of Orion, also known as the Three Kings or Three Sisters, is an asterism in the constellation Orion. It consists of the three bright stars: Alnitak, Alnilam and Mintaka. With precision and an eye to the sky, the great builders of the pyramids replicated the Belt of Orion on the sands of Kemet. From old nile valley writings, the ancient people of wrote that the Neterss descended from the Belt of Orion, which allowed the physical existence of sentient beings.

Orion became associated with the God Osiris, and Sirius associated with the Goddess Isis. Combined, they comprised all of human civilization. According to the ancient tales, Sirius was a gate to other realms, and the pyramids all around the world intentionally align with Orion, forming magical entry and exit ports to other worlds.

In the 1980s, researcher Robert Bauval identified similarities between the topography of the three pyramids of the Giza Complex and the relative separation between the three stars in the constellation of Orion. The theory went viral in Bauval's 1995 New York Times bestseller, The Orion Mystery. In his book, he expands on the rationale that the pyramids were created to serve as a gateway to the stars. Bauval claims that the constellation Orion governs the construction of all the pyramids. His concept became known as the "Orion Correlation Theory" or OCT and asserts that there is a correlation between the location of the three largest pyramids of the Giza Complex and the Orion constellation (pp. 7–18).
Looking for Orion's Belt is the easiest way to locate Orion in the night sky.

(Photo credit: https://catalystmagazine.net/americas-ancient-earthworks/)

(Photo credit: Courtesy of Colorado University)

Myth: Africans did not know astronomy.

Enlightenment: Africans were very familiar with the stars, planets as well as movement of the sun and the Earth. Africans also invented the calendar with days, months and years, based on astronomy.

Khufu Boat

(Photo credit: El Haram, Pyramids Zone, Giza, Kemet)

As an intact, full-size solar barque, the Khufu Ship was sealed into a pit at the foot of the Great Pyramid of King Khufu in the Giza Pyramid Complex around 2500 BCE, during the Fourth Dynasty of the Old Kingdom of Egypt. In accordance with Ancient Kemetic burial rituals, sailing vessels were included in the gravesite goods intended for use in the afterworld.

One of the largest and earliest, the Khufu vessel is the best-preserved ship in the world. The boat is 43.4 meters (142 ft.) in length and 5.9 meters (19 ft.) in width. The boat has been identified as the "world's oldest intact ship" and recognized as an icon mastery of woodcraft that probable could sail today, if it were to enter a river or lake. Initially, Giza Solar Boat Museum preserved it, but since August 2021, the Grand Egyptian Museum stores the Khufu Ship (EI).

Myth: Noah's Ark was the first boat and Christopher Columbus discovered America.

Enlightenment: Africans were not only excellent swimmers, but also they built ships thousands of years before the story of Noah's Ark and before Christopher Columbus came to America. The story of Noah's Ark was fabricated over one thousand years long after the physical existence of the Khufu Boat.

King Djedefre was the son of King Khufu.

(Photo credit, Daniel Laroche, Cairo Museum, Kemet)

In the 4th Dynasty during the Old Kingdom, Djedefre was an Ancient Kemetic pharaoh (Egyptian king). He was the son and throne successor of King Khufu (builder of the Great Pyramid of Giza), but his mother is unknown. Djedefre introduced the royal title Sa-Rê which means "Son of Ra". He was the first pharaoh to attach his Shen name to the sun god Ra. He also was called Djedefra and Radjedef (Verner, p. 375).

(Photo credit: Daniel Laroche, Abydos, Kemet)

(Photo credit: Courtesy of AhlyMan)
The Ruined Pyramid of Djedefre at Abu Rawash

Based on cattle counts, King Djedefre ruled Kemet (Egypt) no less than 11 years, if it was annual, or 22 years, if it was biennial. To construct his pyramid at Abu Rawash, Djedefre decided to go approximately 8 kilometers (5 miles) north of Giza, the northern most area of the Memphite necropolis, and his pyramid complex was finished during his reign. "Natural rock promontory" comprised approximately 45% of the pyramid's core. It was 200 cubits in length and 125 cubits in height but stands no more, now ruined. The original size of Djedefre's pyramid equates to the pyramid volume of Menkaura. Some facts indicate the first sphinx built was that of his wife, Hetepheres II, which also was included in his pyramid complex (Vallogia, p. 418).

In addition, recent evidence strongly suggests that the root cause of the dilapidated monument was because of extensive thievery in later periods. As late as the 2nd century AD, statues of Pharaoh Djedefre were destroyed. Only a small remnant of Djedefre's complex was found because of the poor state of Abu Rawash. With great difficulty, only a rough ground design of his mud brick temple was found on the east side of the pyramid at an usual location. Also, the causeway of King Djedefre's pyramid flowed from north to south rather than the more orthodox east to west; no valley temple ever was located as written in Archaeology News Network.

King Kafre - 2nd Son of Khufu

(Photo credit: Daniel Laroche, MD, Cairo Museum,
Shen, Kafre, Temple of Seti Abydos,Kemet)

King Khafre

(Photo credit: Daniel Laroche, MD, Cairo Museum, Kemet)

(Photo credit: Daniel Laroche, Cairo Museum, Kemet)

Khafre was a Kemetic pharaoh (king) of the 4th Dynasty during the Old Kingdom. He was the son of Khufu and the successor of Djedefre. Khafre was the builder of the second largest pyramid of Giza. Modern Egyptologists hold the view that the Great Sphinx was built in approximately 2500 BCE for Khafre (Wikipedia, "Khafre").

(Photo credit: Daniel Laroche, Cairo, Kemet)

Also known as the solar deity or "Horus of the Horizon", the **Great Sphinx of Giza** in Kemet (Egypt) is distinguished as one of the oldest and most recognizable statues on earth. According to archaeologists, it was created during the Old Kingdom when King Khafre ruled from 2558 – 2532 BCE. Pharaoh Thutmose IV during his reign from 1401–1391 or 1397–1388 BCE, depending on the source, considered it his "Dream Stele".

Standing on the elevated plain of Giza Nile's west bank, the Great Sphinx is a limestone sculpture of a king's head on the resting body of a lion. As a representation of Pharaoh Khafre, this describes man's complete control over his animal self in Kemetic symbolism. The head of the Great Sphinx faces west while the hind tail points east. Originally craved from bedrock, it has been reinforced with layers of limestone blocks. It measures from the paw to the tail 73 meters (240 ft.) in length and from its base to its head top 20 meters (66 ft.) in height with a width of 19 meters (62 ft.) (Wikipedia, "Khafre").

Vesica Piscus with the Sphinx in Front of the Pyramid of Khafre

(Photo source: Public Domain)

The word vesica piscus is Latin, literally meaning the "bladder of a fish". As a type of optical lens, vesica piscus forms a geometrical shape when two spheres with the same radius intersect symmetrically, in which the center of each disk rests on the perimeter of the other. Their forms resemble conjoined dual air bladders or swim bladders that are found in most fish

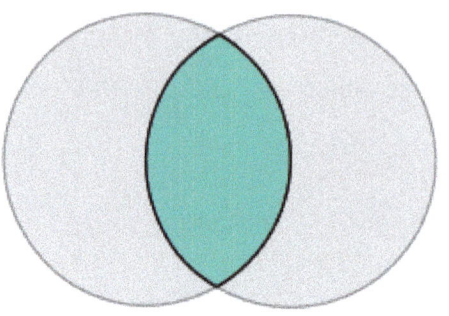

(Photo credit: Courtesy of Tomr)

This originated in Ancient Kemet and was used in many calculations in building structures and in the arts. The Europeans and Americans copied it, which is seen in the Washington Monument in the United States.

Graywacke Statue of King Menkaura with Neter Hathor (left) and Goddess Bat (right)

(Photo credit: Daniel Laroche, Cairo Museum, Kemet)

Also spelled Menkaura, Menkaure was a Kemetic pharaoh (king) of the Fourth Dynasty during the Old Kingdom. He is the male offspring of Khafre and the grandson of Khufu. His pyramid is at Giza and was referred as Netjer-er-Menkaure, which translates as "Menkaure is Divine". As the smallest of three main pyramids at Giza, the pyramid of King Menkaure measures 103.4 meters (339 ft.) at the base and 65.5 meters (215 ft.) in height and has three subsidiary pyramids related (Schneider, pp. 163–164).

The pyramids were built by three generations of Africans: starting with Sneferu and his son Khufu, then followed by Khufu's sons Djedra and Khafre, and finally Khufu's grandson, Menkaure. These pyramids are the only remaining icon of the "Seven Wonders of the World", an amazing engineering feat, father-son-grandson tribute and legacy from the world of African origin.

How were the pyramids built?

At the ancient location of Hatnub, archaeologists recently located a sled ramp apparatus at a quarry in the eastern Kemetic (Egyptian) desert near Faiyum. The stair layer ramp and hole posts suggest that Kemetic (Egyptian) builders used them to transport heavy slabs up and down steep inclines. Reconstruction of the ramp system provides an in-depth insight into Ancient Kemetic construction strategies and dismantles the myth that aliens built the great pyramids of Kemet (Egypt).

What was the diet of the pyramid builders?

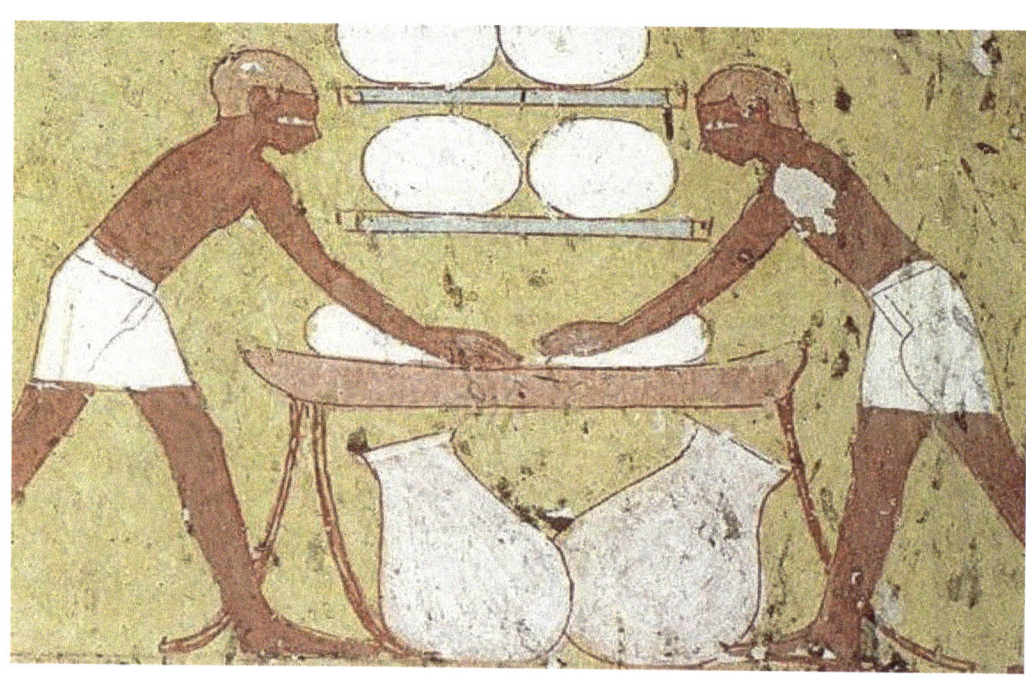

(Photo credit: Courtesy of Historia y Vida)

The labor force comprised of servants who served the pharaoh and charged a fee. They received salaries rendered in rations just as priests, soldiers, and other temple workers. The Ancient Kemetic work force did not receive or know about money but accepted payment as beer and bread, which were their food stables. The rations often consisted of a combined ten daily units. The documents discovered in the Nubian fortress of Ur-onarti revealed the weekly rations of soldiers who secured the southern boundary of Kemet. In Ancient Kemet, a week consisted of 10 days, not seven like today. The ten-day rations were 60 units of cooked barley, estimated at five pounds (2.25 kg), and 70 units of cooked wheat, tallied slightly more than eight pounds (3.75 kg).

These amounts provided them with 2,136 calories a day, which were insufficient. Therefore, cereals could only represent a part of their pay, so rations of beer and some animal proteins had to be added. Without the added calories, the soldiers could not carry out their work of patrolling the desert (Hill, "beer").

Pyramid Builders and Meat Consumption

The discovery of nearly two hundred thousand bones and fragments belonging to fish, birds and mammals confirms the protein intake of the pyramid builders at Giza. Pig bones were the least present while most abundant were bones from young male sheep, goats and cows. Also discovered in the city of the pyramid builders were bakeries and stables. The housing of the builders and the breeding of the cattle were carried out elsewhere. For example, in the settlement of Kom el-Hisn in the Delta, the primary role of certain workers was breeding and fattening of cattle, which meant the kings' court had to increase the protein consumption of the workers. In addition to meat, builders received rations of wheat and barley which were often converted into bread and beer. This was the only way they could reach the more than three thousand daily calories essential to carry out their heavy workload. Evidence of extra rations to perform heavy work is written in the beautification on the tomb of Antefoker, who was in Thebes during the Twelfth Dynasty. Another way the pharaoh paid wages was the distribution of temple offerings, made twice a day.

The writings in the Mortuary Temple of Neferirkare (Fifth Dynasty) show the large volume of protein consumption as 660 birds per month (8,000 a year) and 30 oxen per month (360 a year). After spending a few hours on the altar in feeding the gods substance, the fowl and meat were removed and distributed among all the temple workers, not just the priests. Of course, following a strict hierarchy, the priest received more food than the builders and premium parts, perhaps the oxen skin. This type of distribution was one of the basic exercises that a scribe had to learn, since the proper functioning of the Pharaonic administration depended on it (Verner, Vol. 41, pp. 407– 410).

Two Ancient Kemetic Woman
Making an Offering

![Relief of two ancient Kemetic women making an offering]

(Photo credit: Courtesy of Historia y Vida)

Beer in Ancient Egypt

Heqet – beer

Beer was generally known as "Hqt" ("heqet" or "heket") to Ancient Kemetic people but was also called "tnmw" ("tenemu"). There was a type of beer known as haAmt ("kha-ahmet"), and the word that determined beer (Hqt) was a beer jug.

Haamet – beer

Tenemu – beer

It is no exaggeration to say that water and drinks were of central importance to Ancient Egyptian society. They often made offerings of beer to the Neters, and beer was mentioned in the traditional offering formula. Wages were often paid in beer and other supplies. The workmen living in the worker's village at Giza received beer three times a day as part of their rations (Hill, "beer").

(Photo credit: Courtesy of Ancient Egypt Online)

Evidence indicates as a staple food Ancient Egyptian beer was not particularly intoxicating; rather it was thick as recognized in the festivals of Hathor, Bast and Sekhmet (Hill, "sekhmet").

An Offering Table Depicting Beer Jugs

(Photo credit: Egyptian - Offering Table - Walters 22136.jpg)

The main ingredient in the beer was bread made from rich yeasty dough, possibly including malt. The bread was lightly baked and crumbled into small pieces before being strained through a sieve with water. Flavor was added in the form of dates, and the mixture was fermented in a large vat and then stored (Hill, "beer").

(Photo credit: Courtesy of Ancient Egypt Online)

Evidence also suggests that beer was brewed from barley and emmer, which was heated and mixed with yeast and uncooked malt before being fermented to produce beer. Beer also appears prominently in Kemetic literature and sayings. For example, in this inscription dated around 2200 BCE, it says, "The mouth of a perfectly contented man is filled with beer" (Hill, "beer").

Facts: Ptahhotep (2405 – 2367 BCE) was the "Chief Justice and Vizier of King Djedkare Isesi". In numerous portrayals, he is depicted with different hairstyles and belts, perhaps representing different stages of his life or his various official roles. He is also the author of the world's oldest completed book, The Maxims of Ptahhotep. This book provides instructions on leadership and ethical standards for his son (Fontaine, vol. 44, no. 3, pp. 155–160).

Images at the Tomb of Ptahhotep

(Photo credit: Daniel Laroche, Saqqara, Kemet)

(Photo credit: Daniel Laroche, Saqqara, Kemet)

(Photo credit: Daniel Laroche, Saqqara, Kemet)

(Photo credits: Daniel Laroche, Saqqara, Kemet)

(Photo credit: Daniel Laroche, Imhotep Museum, Saqqara, Kemet)

(Photo credit: Daniel Laroche, Imhotep Museum, Saqqara, Kemet)

THE QUOTED TEACHINGS OF PTAHHOTEP

(An African father leaving lessons for his son in 2400 BCE)

1. *Do not be proud and arrogant with your knowledge. Consult and converse with the ignorant and the wise, for the limits of art are not reached. No artist ever possesses that perfection to which he should aspire; good speech is more hidden than greenstone [emeralds], yet it may be found among maids at the grindstone.*

2. *If you meet a disputant in the heat of action, one who is more power-ful than you, simply fold your arms and bend your back. To confront him will not make him agree with you. Pay no attention to his evil speech. If you do not confront him while he is raging, people will call him an igno-ramus. Your self- control will be the match for his evil utterance.*

3. *If you meet a disputant in action, one who is your equal, one who is on your level, you will overcome him by being silent while he is speak-ing evilly. There will be much talk among those who hear, and your name will be held in high regard among the great.*

4. *If you meet a disputant in action who is a poor man and who is not your equal do not attack him because he is weak. Leave him alone. He will confound himself. Do not vent yourself against your opponent. Wretched is he who injures a poor man. If you ignore him, listeners will wish to do what you want. You will beat him through their reproof.*

5. *If you are a man who leads a man who controls the affairs of many, then seek the most perfect way of performing your responsibility so that your conduct will be blameless. Great is Maat (truth, justice and righ-*

teousness). It is everlasting. Maat has been unchanged since the time of Asar. To create obstacles to the following of laws is to open a way to a condition of violence. The transgressor of laws is punished, although the greedy person over-looks this. Baseness may obtain riches, yet crime never lands its wares on the shore. In the end only Maat lasts. Man says, "Maat is my father's ground."

6.   Do not scheme against people. God will punish; accordingly, if a man says, "I shall live by scheming," he will lack bread for his mouth. If a man says, "I will be rich;" he will have to say, "my cleverness has trapped me." If he says," I will trap for myself," he will not be able to say, "I trapped for my profit." If a man says, "I will rob someone," he will end by being given to a stranger. People's schemes do not prevail. Therefore, live in the midst of peace. What God gives come by itself?

7.   If you are among guests at the table of a person who is more powerful than you, take what that person gives just as it is set before you. Don't stare at your host. Don't speak to him until he asks. One does not know what may displease him. Speak when he has spoken to you. Then your words will please the heart. The man who has plenty of the means of existence acts as his Ka [soul] commands. He will give food to those who he favors. It is the Ka that makes his hands stretch out. The great man gibes to the chosen man; thus, eating is under the direction of God. It is a fool who complains about it.

8.   If you are a person of trust sent by one great person, be careful to stick to the essence of the message that you were asked to transmit. Give the message exactly as he gave it to you. Guard against provocative speech which makes one great person angry with another. Just keep to the truth. Do not exceed it. However, even though they may

have been an out-burst in the message you should not repeat it. Do not malign anyone, great or small, the Ka abhors it.

9. If you plow and if there is growth in your field and God lets it prosper in your hand, don't boast to your neighbor. One has great respect for the silent person. A person of character is a person of wealth. If that person robs, he or she is like a crocodile in the middle of the waters. If God gives you children, don't impose on one who has no children. Neither should you decry or brag about having your own children, for there is many a father who has grief and many a mother with children who is less content than another. It is the lonely whom God nurtures while the family man prays for a follower.

10. If you are poor, then serve a person of worth so that your conduct may be well with God. Do not bring up the fact that he was once poor. Do not be arrogant towards him just because you know about his former state. Respect him now for his position of authority. As for fortune, it obeys its own law and who makes him worthy and who protects him while he sleeps, of who can turn away from him.

11. Follow your heart as long as you live. Do no more than is required. Do not shorten the time of "follow the heart", since that offence the Ka. Don't waste time on daily cares over and beyond providing for your household. When wealth finally comes, then follow your heart. Wealth does no good if you are glum.

12. If you are a wise man, train up a son who will be pleasing to God. If he is straight and takes after you, take good care of him. Do everything that is good for him. He is your son, your Ka begot him. Don't withdraw your heart from him. But an offspring can make trouble. If your son strays and neglects your council and disobeys all that is said, with his

mouth spouting evil speech, then punish him for all his talk. God will hate him who crosses you. His guilt was determined in the womb.

13. If you are a guard in the storehouse, stand or sit rather than leave your post and trespass into someone else's place. Follow this rule from the first. Never leave your post, even when fatigued. Keen is the face to him enters announced, and spacious is the seat of him who has been asked to come in; the store house has fixed rules. All behavior is strictly by the rule. Only a God can penetrate the secure warehouse where the rules are followed, even by privileged persons.

14. If you are among the people, then gain your supporters by building trust. The trusted man is one who does not speak the first thing that comes to mind, and he will become a leader. A man of means has a good name, and his face is benign. People will praise him even without his knowledge. On the other hand, he whose heart obeys his belly asks for contempt of himself in the unanimated. The great hearted is a gift of God. He who is ruled by his appetite belongs to the enemy.

15. Report the thing that you were commissioned to report without error. Give your advice in the high council. If you are fluent in your speech, it will not be hard for you to report. Nor will anyone say of you, "who is he to know this?" As to the authorities, their affairs will fail if they punish you for speaking truth. They should be silent upon hearing the report that you have rendered as you have been told. If you are a man who leads, a man whose authority reaches widely, then you should do perfect things, those which posterity will remember. Don't listen to the words of flatterers of words that puff you up with pride and vanity.

16. If you are a person who judges, listen carefully of the speech of one who pleads. Don't stop the person from telling you everything that they

had planned to tell you. A person in distress wants to pour out his or her heart, even more than they want their case to be won. If you are one who stops a person who is pleading, that person will say, "why does he reject my plea?" Of course, not all that one pleads for can be granted, but a good hearing soothes the heart. The means for getting a true and clear explanation is to listen with kindness.

17.   If you want friendship to endure in the house that you enter, the house of a master, of a brother or a friend, then in whatever place you enter beware of approaching the woman there. Unhappy is the place where this is done. Unwelcome is he who intrudes on them. A thousand men are turned away from their good because of a short moment that is like a dream, and then that moment is followed by death that comes from having known that dream. Anyone who encourages taking advantage of the situation gives you poor advice. When you go to do it, your heart says no. If you are one who fails through the lust of women, then no affair of yours can prosper.

18.   If you want to have perfect conduct, to be free from every evil, then above all guard against the vice of greed. Greed is a grievous sickness that has no cure. There is no treatment for it. It embroils father, mothers and the brothers of the mother. It parts the wife from the husband. Greed is a compound of all evils. It is a bundle of all hateful things. That person endures whose rule is rightness, who walks a straight line, for that person will leave a legacy by such behavior. On the other hand, the greedy has no tomb.

19.   Do not be greedy in the division of things. Do not covet more than your share. Don't be greedy towards your relatives. A mild person has greater claim than the harsh one. Poor is the person who forgets his

relatives. He is deprived of their company. Even a little bit of what is wanted to turn a quarreler into a friendly person.

20.　When you prosper and establish your home, love your wife with ardor. Then fill her belly and clothe her back. Caress her. Give her ointments to soothe her body. Fulfill her wishes for as long as you live. She is a fertile field for her husband. Do not be brutal. Good manners will influence her better than force. Do not content with her in the courts. Keep her from the need to resort to outside powers. Her eye is her storm when she gazes. It is by such treatment that she will be compelled to stay in your house.

21.　Help your friends with things that you have, for you have these things by the grace of God. If you fail to help your friends, one will say you have a selfish Ka. One plans for tomorrow, but you do not know what tomorrow will bring. The right soul is the soul by which one is sustained. If you do praiseworthy, your friend will say, "welcome" in your time of need. Don't repeat slander nor should you even listen to it. It is the spouting of the hot bellied. Just report a thing that has been observed, not something that has been heard secondhand. If it's something negligible, don't even say anything. He who standing before you will recognize your worth. Slander is like a terrible dream against which one covers the face.

22.　If you are a man of worth who sits at the council of a leader, concentrate on being excellent. Your silence is much better than boasting. Speak when you know that you have a solution. It is the skilled person who should speak when in council. Speaking is harder than all other work. The one who understands this makes speech a servant.

23.　If you are mighty and powerful, then gain respect through knowledge

112

and through your gentleness of speech. Don't order a thing except as it is fitting. The one who provokes others get into trouble. Don't be haughty lest you be humble. But also, don't be mute lest you be chided. When you answer one who is fuming, turn your face and control yourself. The flame of the hot hearted sweeps across everything. But he who steps gently, his path is paved road. He who is agitated all day has no happy moments but who amuses himself all day can't keep his fortune.

24. Do not disturb a great man or distract his attention when he is occupied, trying to understand his task. When he is thus occupied, he strips his body through the love of what he does. Love for the work which they do brings men closer to God. These are the people who succeed in what they do.

25. Teach the great what is useful to them. Be an aide to the great before them. If you let your knowledge impress your leader, your sustenance from him then will come from his soul. As his favorite's belly is filled, so will your back be clothed, and his help will be there to sustain you. For your leader whom you love and who lives by useful knowledge, he in turn will give you good support. Thus, will the love of you endure in his belly? He is a soul who loves to listen.

26. If you are an official of high standing, and you are commissioned to satisfy the many, then hold to a straight line. When you speak don't lean to one side or the other. Beware lest someone complain, saying to the judges, "he has distorted things", and then your very deeds will turn into a judgment of you.

27. If you are angered by a misdeed, then lean toward a man on account of his rightness. Pass over the misdeed and don't remember it since God was silent to you on the first day of your misdeed.

28.   If you are great after having been humble, if you have gained your wealth after having been poor, then go to a town that you know and that knows your former condition; don't put your trust in your newly acquired wealth which has come to you as a gift of God. If you do, one day someone there who is poor may very well overtake you.

29.   Accept the authority of your leaders then your house will endure in its wealth. Your rewards will come from the right place. Wretched is he who opposes his leader. One lives as long as he is mind. Baring your arm does not hurt it. Do not plunder your neighbor's house or steal the goods of one that is near you, lest he denounce you before you are even heard. One who is argumentative is a mild less person. If he is also known as an aggressor, then that hostile man will have trouble in the neighborhood.

30.   Be circumspect in matters of sexual relations.

31.   If you examine the character of a friend, don't ask other people, approach your friend. Deal with him alone, so as not to suffer from his anger. You may argue with him after a little while. You may test his heart in conversation. If what he has seen escapes him, if he does something that annoys you, stay friendly with him and do not attack. Be restrained and don't answer him with hostility. Do not leave him and do not attack him. His time will not fail to come. He cannot escape his fate.

32.   Be generous as long as you live. What leaves the storehouse does not return. It is the food in the storehouse that one must share that is coveted. One whose belly is empty becomes an accuser. One who is deprived becomes an opponent. Therefore, do not have an accuser or an opponent as a neighbor. Your kindness to your neighbors will be memorial to you for years, after you satisfy their needs.

33. *Know your friends and then you prosper. Don't be mean towards your friends. They are like a watered field and greater than any material riches that you may have, for what belongs to another. The character of one who is well born be a profit to him. Good nature is a memorial.*

34. *Punish firmly and chastise soundly, then repression of crime becomes an example. But punishment expect for the crime will turn the complainer into an enemy.*

35. *If you take for a wife a good time woman who is joyful and who is well known in the town, if she is fickle and seems to live for the moment, do not reject her. Let her eat. The joyful person brings happiness.*

36. *If you listen to my saying, all of your affairs will go forward. Their value resides in their worth of percepts. If every word is carried on, they will not perish in this land. If advice is given for the good, the great will speak accordingly. This is a matter of teaching a person to speak posterity. He or she who hears it becomes a master hearer. It is good to speak posterity. Posterity will listen.*

37. *If an example is set by him or her who leads, he or she will be beneficent forever, his wisdom lasting for all time. The person feeds the Ka with what endures, so that it is happy with that person on earth. The wise is known by his good actions. The heart of the wise matches his or her tongue and his or her lips are straight when he or she speaks. The wise have eyes that are made to see and ears that are made to hear what the profit offspring will. The wise person who acts with the Maat is free of falsehood and disorder.*

38. *Useful is hearing to a son who hears. If hearing enters the hearer,*

then the hearer becomes a listener. Hearing well is speaking well. Useful is hearing to one who hears. Hearing is better than everything else. It creates good will. How good it is for a son to understand his father's words. That son will reach old age through those words.

39.   He who hears is beloved of God. He whom God hates does not hear. The heart makes of its owner a hearer or a non-hearer. Man's heart in his life, prosperity, and health. The hearer is one who hears what is said. He who loves to hear is one who acts on what is said. How good it is for a son to listen to his father. How happy he is to whom it is said "Your son is a master of hearing." The hearers of whom this is said well-endowed indeed and is honored by his father. That hearer's remembrance is in the mouth of the living, those that are on earth and those who will be.

40.   If a man's son accepts his father words, then no plan of his will go wrong. So, teach your son to be a hearer, one who will be valued by the officials, one who will guide his speech by what he has been told, and one who is regarded as a hearer. This son will excel, and his deeds will stand out while failure will follow those who do not hear. The wise wakes up early to his lasting gain while the fool is hard pressed.

41.   The fool who does not hear, he can do nothing at all. He looks at ignorance and sees knowledge. He looks at harmfulness and sees usefulness. He does everything that one detests and is blamed for it every day. He lives on the things by which one dies. His food is evil speech. His sort is known to the officials who say, "There goes a living death

every day." One ignores the things that he does because of his many daily troubles. A son who hears is a follower of HERU. When he is old and has reached the period where he is venerated, then he will speak likewise to his own children, renewing then the teachings of his father.

42. Every man teaches as he acts. He will speak to the children so that they will speak to their children. He will set an example and not give offense. So if justice stands firm, your children will live. As to the first child who gets into trouble, when people see it, they will say about that child "that is just like him", and they will also say when they even hear a rumor about the child, "that is just like him too."

43. To see everyone is to satisfy the many. Any riches that you have are useless without the many. Don't say something and then take it back. Don't put one thing in place of another. Beware of releasing the restraints in you, least the wise man says, "listen, if you want to endure in the mouth of the hearers, speak after you have master the craft." If you speak to good purpose, all your affairs will be in place.

44. Conceal your heart. Control your mouth. Then you will be known among the officials. Be ````quite exact before your leader. Act so that no one will say to him, "he is the son of that one."

45. Be deliberate when you speak to say things that count. Then the officials who listen will say, "How good is the thing that comes from his mouth." Act so that your leader will say of you, "how good is he whom his father has taught. When comes forth from his body, he told him all that was in his mind, and he does even more than he was told."

46. The good son is the gift of God and exceeds what is told him by his leader. He will do right when his heart is straight. As you succeed me sound in the body, a Pharaoh, content with all that was done, may you

obtain many years of life.

47. *The things that I did on earth were not small. I have had 110 years of life. As a gift of the Pharaoh, I have had honors exceeding those of the ancestors, by doing Maat until the state of veneration.*

48. *It is done, from this beginning to its end, as it was found in the writings of the ancestors and Deity.*

Myth: When people of African descent read and write, they are acting white.

Enlightenment: The teachings of Ptahhotep are important for many reasons. We may note among these reasons that they provide a glimpse of a profound way of life based on intellectual and spiritual teaching that guided ancient Africans. Ptahhotep, therefore, laid no claim to the original authorship. His wisdom was that of his people and the Deity.

Comparing the wisdom teachings of Ptahhotep to the Mesopotamian Code of Hammurabi which was developed many centuries later, we may find toleration for slavery, if not an entire justification for it. Ptahhotep and other scribe priests taught a supremely democratic and humane system of thought. The study of Ptahhotep teachings and other Ancient Kemetic, sacred texts is essential to an understanding both of Africa and the development of the world, in particular "western civilization".

Unity of culture between Kemet and its sister nations of Africa existed. Thus, these teachings do not merely illuminate the mind of Ptahhotep and the Kemetic ways of life. They illuminate general African culture from ancient times to the present. Using indigenous African literature, we can once again share this humane, democratic, and deeply spiritual ways of life with the world.

Offering Procession of Two Men with Canopy Jars, Lotus and Papyrus as Part of a Funeral Ritual

(Photo credit: Daniel Laroche, Metropolitan Museum)

Facts: The Pyramid Complex of Djedkare Isesi was built for the Fifth Dynasty Pharaoh Djedkare Isesi and was the first pyramid built in South His name means "Beautiful is Djedkare.

The pyramid complex includes a main pyramid, a mortuary temple on the east face of the main pyramid, a valley temple buried under modern Saqqara, and a partially dug out causeway. The main pyramid is a six-stepped core, built from rough-cut limestone, bound by clay mortar, and encased in fine white Tura limestone. The monument reaches a peak height of 52.5 meters or 172 ft. (100.2 cubic units). Since the casing of the main core was stolen, the pyramid stands a 24 meters or 79 ft. (46 cubic units) tall.

Attached to the east face of the pyramid is the mortuary temple. Neighboring the entrance passageway to the temple are two large pylon constructions. A large structure with several long narrow rooms was discovered west of the south pylon building. Foundational blocks were used in preserving the outer area of the structure.

Inside the substructure of the pyramid are the mummy remains of Djedkare Isesi himself. The mummy and linen wrapping underwent Carbon-14 dating, which reveals a common range of 2886 – 2507 BCE. Stone robbers, quarrying the Tura limestone casing, badly damaged the substructure of the pyramid (Verner).

Tomb of Djedkare at Saqqara

(Photo credit: Mohamed Megahed, Archaeological Institute of America)

Tomb of Djedkare Saqqara

(Photo credit: Mohamed Megahed, Archaeological Institute of America)

Pyramid of Djedkare

(Photo credit: https://en.wikipedia.org/wiki/Pyramid_of_Djedkare_Isesi)

121

Tomb of Djedkare

(Photo Credits: Mohamed el-Shahed, Agence France Presse)

The Ancient Nile valley builders of the great pyramids possibly wet the sand in front of a device to move the enormous stone blocks.

Dating back approximately to 1900 BCE, a wall painting discovered in the tomb of Djehutihotep illustrates 172 engineers transporting a massive statue, using cords attached to a sled. In the drawing, a worker, kneeling in front of the sleigh, pours a liquid over the earth. Researchers investigated this theory and found when pulling an oversized sled across dry sand, it clumps, which would have meant the builders had to increase the amount of force to move the humongous stones across the desert. The droplets from the added water produced bridges between the grains of sand and stiffened the surface in order that the sleigh glided more easily across the ground (Chow).

Djehutihotep Painting of Builders Moving Stones

(Photo credit: Courtesy of Archaeology.wiki)

Myth: Africans contributed nothing to civilization.

Enlightenment: Africans founded civilization.

Volume 1 References

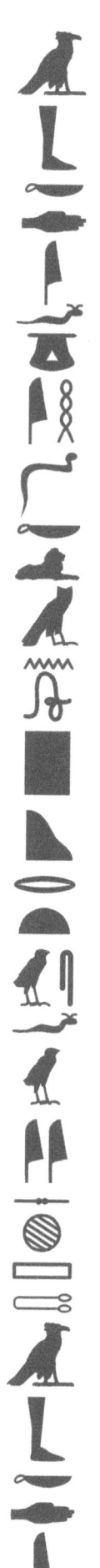

Ahmed, Mona. "Nubia's bittersweet memories behind High Dam." egypttoday.com, 27 Nov 2017, https://www.egypttoday.com/Article/6/34353/Nubia%E2%80%99s-bittersweet-memories-behind-High-Dam. Accessed 21 Mar. 2022.

Alchin, Linda. "The Uraeus Symbol." Egyptian Gods. Siteseen Ltd, n.d. Web.

"Archaeologists Uncover 4,500-Year-Old Ramp System at Alabaster Quarry in Egypt." SciNews.
    7 Nov 2018. https://www.sci.news/archaeology/ramp-system-alabaster-quarry-egypt-06582.html. Accessed 28 Jan. 2023.

Bard, K.A. Encyclopedia of the Archaeology of Ancient Egypt. Routledge Publishing, 1999.

Bauval, Robert G. "Orion Correlation Theory or OCT." Discussions in Egyptology (DE), Vol. 13, 1989, pp. 7-18.

Beaumont, Peter B. South African Journal of Science, "Border Cave: Progress Report." 1973.

"Bent Pyramid." 30 Nov 2022. wikipedia.org, Wikipedia. https://en.wikipedia.org/wiki/Bent_Pyramid. Accessed 26 Dec. 2022.

The Book of the Dead. Specialty Book Marketing Inc. and Studio 31, 2015, pp. 97– 96.

Budge, Wallis E. A. Budge's Egypt: A Classical 19th-Century Travel Guide. Dover Publications, 16 Jul 2022.

Chow, Denise. "Solved! How Ancient Egyptians Moved Massive Pyramid Stones." LiveScience, 1 May 2014. https://www.livescience.com/45285-how-egyptians-moved-pyramid-stones.html. Accessed 20 Mar. 2022.

"Could Djedefre's Pyramid Be A Solar Temple?." archaeonewsnet.com, Archaeology News Network. 3 May 2010. Accessed 28 Jul. 2022.

Darling, David. The Universal Book of Mathematics. Wiley Publishing, 1

Aug 2004.

"Djoser." 7 Dec 2022. wikipedia.org, Wikipedia. 7 June 2022. https://en.wikipedia.org/wiki/Djoser. Accessed 21 Dec. 2022.

Dorman, Peter F. & Faulkner, Raymond O. "Ramses II." 25 Oct 2022. britannica.com, Britannica. https://www.britannica.com/place/ancient-Egypt/Ramses-IIhttps://www.britannica.com/place/ancient-Egypt/Ramses-II. Accessed 18 Jan. 2023.

Dr. Y. "Lucy: the Oldest Ancestor to Mankind?." afrolegends.com, African Heritage. 1 Sept 2021, https://afrolegends.com/tag/dinkinesh/. Accessed 26 Jun. 2022.

El, Nash. "The secrets of ancient 'Solar Boat' unearthed at Khufu pyramid." Mysteries Unsolved, 18 Sept 2022, https://mysteriesrunsolved.com/2022/09/the-secrets-of-ancient-solar-boat-unearthed-at-khufu-pyramid.html. Accessed 8 Mar. 2023.

El-Shahawy, Abeer. The Funerary Art of Ancient Egypt: A Bridge to the Realm of the Hereafter. American University Press, 2005, p.106.

Fontaine, Carole R. "A Modern Look at Ancient Wisdom: The Instruction of Ptahhotep Revisited." The Biblical Archaeologist, vol. 44, no. 3, 1981, pp. 155–160.

Frankfort, Henri. Ancient Egyptian Religion: An Interpretation. "The Instruction of Ptahhotep," Dover Publications, 2011, p. 62.

Guido, Montelupo, editor. Ani. The Egyptian Book of the Dead: The Papyrus of Ani. Scotts Valley: Create Space Independent Publishing Platform, 2014.

Hayes, Michael. The Cambridge Ancient History, Volume I, Part I, Page 24, Chapter VI, "Chronology I, Egypt to the end of the Twentieth Dynasty." Edwards, I.E.S.; Gadd, C.J. (eds.). Cambridge Publishing, 1970.

"Hesy-Ra." 19 Nov 2022. wikipedia.org, Wikipedia. https://en.wikipedia.org/wiki/Hesy-Ra. Accessed 21 Nov. 2022.

Hill, Jenny. "beer." 2010. ancientegyptonline.co.uk, Ancient Egypt Online, "Daily Life in Ancient Egypt," ch 9. https://ancientegyptonline.co.uk/beer/. Accessed 20 Nov. 2022.

Hill, Jenny. "Westcar Papyrus." Translated by Marc Jan Nederhof & A.M. Blackman. ancientegyptonline.co.uk, Ancient Egypt Online, 2008. https://ancientegyptonline.co.uk/westcar-papyrus/. Accessed 20 Nov. 2022.

Hilliard, Asa. "The Master Keys to Study Ancient Kemet" Interview with Lestervelt Middleton, Lestervelt Middleton TV Show, Waset Educational Productions, East Point, GA, 19 June 2015, https://www.youtube.com/watch?v=9xkjsq4u-LY. Accessed 26 Mar. 2022.

Hurry, Imhotep J.B. The Vizier and Physician of King Zoser and Afterwards the Egyptian God of Medicine. Oxford University Press, 1926.

"Imhotep." 19 Jan 2023. britannica.com, Britannica. 7 Jul 2022. https://www.britannica.com/biography/Imhotep. Accessed 20 Jan. 2023.

Karenga, Maulana. Maat, The Moral Ideal in Ancient Egypt: A Study in Classical African Ethics, University of Sankore Press, 2006, p.38.

"Khafre." 17 Nov 2022. wikipedia.org, Wikipedia. https://en.wikipedia.org/wiki/Khafre. Accessed 20 Feb. 2023.

"Khufu." 19 Dec 2022. wikipedia.org, Wikipedia. https://en.wikipedia.org/wiki/Khufu. Accessed 2 Feb. 2023.

"Khufu." 18 Feb 2023. wikiwand.com, Wikiwand. https://www.wikiwand.com/en/Khufu. Accessed 27 Feb. 2022.

Kinnaer, Jacques. "Funerary-complex." ancient-egypt.org, The Ancient Egypt Site, 26 Jul 2018, http://www.ancient-egypt.org/history/early-dynastic-period/3rd-dynasty/horus-netjerikhet/funerary-complex/step-pyramid.html. Accessed 13 Jul. 2022.

Kinnaer, Jacques. "History of Ancient Egypt." ancient-egypt.org, The Ancient Egypt Site. 26 Jan 2023, https://ancient-egypt.org/. Accessed 13 Jul. 2022.

Kinnaer, Jacques. "The Narmer Palette." ancient-egypt.org, The Ancient Egypt Site. 17 Jul 2017, http://www.ancient-egypt.org/history/early-dynastic-period/1st-dynasty/horus-narmer/narmer-artefacts/narmer-palette.html. Accessed 13 Jul. 2022.

Leprohon, Ronald J. The Great Name: Ancient Egyptian Royal Titulary. Society of Biblical Literature, 2013.

Lichtheim, Miriam. Ancient Egyptian Literature, Volume I: The New Kingdom. "Utterances 373 & 304" University of California Press, 1975.

Lichtheim, Miriam. Ancient Egyptian Literature, Volume II: The New Kingdom. University of California Press, 1976.

M. Verner, Baugraffiti der Ptahscepses-Mastaba, Praha 1992.

"Maat." 8 Feb 2023. www.wikipedia.org, Wikipedia. 7 Jun 2022. https://en.wikipedia.org/wiki/Maat. Accessed 5 Mar. 2023.

Mark, Joshua J. "Ancient Egyptian Architecture." worldhistory.org, World History Encyclopedia. 18 Sept 2016, https://www.worldhistory.org/Egyptian_Architecture/. Accessed 30 Sept. 2022.

Mark, Joshua J. "Punt." worldhistory.org, World History Encyclopedia. 1 Aug 2011, https://www.worldhistory.org/punt/. Accessed 16 Apr. 2022.

"Meidum." 10 Feb 2023. wikipedia.org, Wikipedia. https://en.wikipedia.org/wiki/Meidum. Accessed 5 Mar. 2023.

"Menkaure." 11 Dec 2022. wikipedia.org, Wikipedia. https://en.wikipedia.org/wiki/Pyramid_of_Menkaure. Accessed 22 Dec. 2022.

Michel Vallogia, Études sur l'Ancien Empire et la nécropole de Saqqara (Fs Lauer) 1997. p.418

Morenz, Siegfried. Egyptian Religion. Cornell University Press, 1973, p. 273.

Newton, Ivy. Africa Factbook, "Story of Ausar, Aset, and Heru." 2008, https://www.theafricangourmet.com/2018/11/story-of-ausar-aset-and-heru.html. Accessed 19 Mar. 2023.

"Palermo Stone." 31 Aug 2022. wikipedia.org, Wikipedia. https://en.wikipedia.org/wiki/Palermo_Stone. Accessed 23 Sept. 2022.

Pinch, Geraldine. Egyptian Mythology: A Guide to the Gods, Goddesses, and Traditions of Ancient Egypt. Oxford University Press, 2002.

"Pyramid Texts." 15 Jan 2023. wikipedia.org, Wikipedia. https://en.wikipedia.org/wiki/Pyramid_Texts. Accessed 23 Jan. 20223.

"Pyramid of Unas." 22 Oct 2022. wikipedia.org, Wikipedia. https://en.wikipedia.org/wiki/Pyramid_of_Unas. Accessed 12 Nov. 2022.

Redford, Donald B. & Meltzer, Edmund S., editors. The Oxford Guide: Essential Guide to Egyptian Mythology". Berkley Press, 2003, pp. 164–168.

"Sah." 26 Sept 2022. wikipedia.org, Wikipedia. https://en.wikipedia.org/wiki/Sah_(god). Accessed 20 Jan. 2023.

Samuel, Alan E. & Dorman, Peter F. "The Predynastic and Early Dynastic period." bitannica.com, 3 Jan 2023, https://www.britannica.com/place/ancient-Egypt/The-Predynastic-and-Early-Dynastic-periods. Accessed 20 Mar. 2023.

Schneider, Thomas. Lexikon der Pharaonen. Albatros, Düsseldorf. 2002, pp. 163-164.

"Scorpion II." 2 Feb 2023. wikipedia.org, Wikipedia. 7 Jun 2022. https://en.wikipedia.org/wiki/Scorpion_II. Accessed 13 Mar. 2023.

Shaltout, Belmonte. "On the Orientation of Ancient Egyptian Temples: (1) Upper Egypt and Lower Nubia." Journal for the History of Astronomy, 1 Aug 2005, 36 (3): pp. 273–298.

Shaw, Ian, editor. The Oxford History of Ancient Egypt. Oxford University Press. 19 Feb 2004.

Smith, Homer W. Man and His Gods. Grosset & Dunlap, 1952, p. 45.

"Sneferu." 30 Dec 2022. wikipedia.org, Wikipedia. https://en.wikipedia.org/wiki/Sneferu. Accessed 18 Mar. 2023.

Strudwick, Helen. The Encyclopedia of Ancient Egypt. Sterling Publishing Co, Inc., 2006, pp. 106–107.

Vallogia, Michel. Études sur l'Ancien Empire et la nécropole de Saqqara (FS Lauer)." Menkaura, 1997, p. 418.

Verner, Miroslav. "Archaeological Remarks on the 4th and 5th Dynasty Chronology." Archiv Orientální, Vol. 69, 2001, p. 375.

Verner, Miroslav. The Pyramids: The Mystery, Culture and Science of Egypt's Great Monuments. Grove Press, 2001.

Verner, Miroslav. "Studien zur Altägyptischen Kultur." Pyramid towns of Abusir, vol. 414, pp. 07–410, 2012, https://www.jstor.org/e/41812236?searchText=41812236&-searchUri=%2Faction%2FdoBasicSearch%3FQuery%3D41812236&ab_seg-ments=0%2Fbasic_search_gsv2%2Fcontrol&refreqid=fastly-default%3A7591d-ba63a89bd971da5a62382b7784c. Accessed 20 Mar. 2022.

Museum Acknowledgment:
    Cairo Museum, Egypt (Kemet)
    Imhotep Museum, Saqqara, Egypt (Kemet)
    Louvre Museum, Ancient Egypt collection, France
    Metropolitan Museum, Ancient Egypt (Kemet) section, New York
    National Museum of Ethiopia, Ethiopia
    Nubian Museum, Aswan Egypt (Kemet)
    Oriental Institute Museum, Ancient Egypt section, Chicago
    Petrie Museum of Egyptian Archeology, London
    Royal Belgian Institute of Natural Sciences, Belgium

*****Special Thanks to Konshu Nok, Jabari Osaze,
and Anika Daniel Osaze*****